field guide to the

APOCALYPSE

Movie Survival Skills for the End of the World

field guide to the APOCALYPSE

Movie Survival Skills for the End of the World

by meghann marco

Illustrated by Dominic Bugatto

SIMON SPOTLIGHT ENTERTAINMENT

New York London Toronto Sydney

SIMON SPOTLIGHT ENTERTAINMENT
An imprint of Simon & Schuster
1230 Avenue of the Americas, New York, New York 10020

Designed by Joel Avirom and Jason Snyder

Manufactured in the United States of America

First Edition 10 9 8 7 6 5 4 3 2 1

Library of Congress Cataloging-in-Publication Data
Marco, Meghann.
Field guide to the Apocalypse / by Meghann Marco ;
illustrated by Dominick Bugatto.— 1st ed.
p. cm.
Includes bibliographical references.
ISBN 0-689-87877-X
1. Millennialism—Humor. 2. End of the world—Humor. I. Title.
PN6231.M52M37 2005 818'.602—dc22 2005003764

contents

PART III:

the advanced technological dystopia

PART IV:

apocalypse then: tips for saving the world

introduction:
what apocalypse?

I kind of like it when a lot of people die.

—GEORGE CARLIN, *NAPALM & SILLY PUTTY*

We're all going to die. You, me, the cat—everybody. The trick is not all dying at the same time. And there are plenty of ways that we could all go. Some of my favorites include:

- A huge fucking meteor smashing into Pennsylvania Amish Country

- That "supervolcano" in Yellowstone National Park that they don't want us to be concerned about

- A virus that makes you eat yourself

- Global thermonuclear war—who knows who has what bombs now?

- And, of course, the sun randomly going supernova

And did you know that we're heading, at over a million miles an hour, toward an unknown object in the constellation Leo? They call it the Great Attractor. They don't know what it is. It could be Rob Lowe, but it's probably a huge black hole that's massive enough to swallow the entire Milky Way.

So there are a lot of ways we could all go. That's not really what this book is about. This book is more concerned with the few people who manage to survive an apocalyptic event. What is considered an apocalyptic event? Any of the above will qualify (minus the whole "black hole swallowing the universe" thing—that doesn't leave much room for books). Here are some more examples:

- **Significant Population Loss:** If we don't have enough people to sustain the economy, civilization will fall.

- **Severe Climate Change:** Global warming, nuclear winter, meteor strike, and/or supervolcanoes—all of these could cause another ice age.

- **Scarcity:** As you'll remember from twelfth-grade economics, scarcity drives up prices. Unfortunately, if that price is for fossil fuels or food, civilization might not be able to adapt quickly enough to save itself.

- **Rampant Technology:** Technology could progress beyond the point that we are able to control it. That would be bad for us.

Thankfully, the great writers, artists, and philosophers of our time have already figured out most of the hard stuff for us. They've told us what might happen, what probably will happen, and what almost certainly won't happen. And then someone took all the great stuff and made a movie or two. For example:

The movie *Blade Runner* predicts that by 2019 almost all living animals will be clones—due to mass extinction caused by human carelessness.

This might sound preposterous to you, but take a moment and consider that on January 4, 2004, the journal *Nature* released a study predicting that within the next fifty years, as many as 37 percent of the world's species will be extinct due to global warming. A few weeks later *Fortune* magazine released an article warning that, according to new data, we could be plunged into the next ice age as early as 2014.

With those two things in mind, the timeline of *Blade Runner* seems more unoptimistic than absurd.

Another good example:

In the *Mad Max* films the United States invaded the Middle East and started the Apocalyptic Oil War in 2003.

This is not a good sign.

But what can we do? Now that we have not heeded the warnings, how do we deal with the reality? Assuming one survives the breakdown of civilization, what skills, tips, and techniques will the average human need to survive in the postapocalyptic landscape? How will you find food, fuel, companionship, and really cool sunglasses? Are you prepared to defend your home against heavily armed and plague-infested zombies? Do you know how to cook SPAM? Are you prepared to cope in a society with no justice system, no television, no Fruit Roll-Ups?

To be helpful, I've broken down the relevant skills into several categories based on the type of apocalypse you may find yourself in. They are:

THE FALSE UTOPIA: Popularized by such works as Aldous Huxley's *Brave New World*, George Orwell's *1984*, and Ray Bradbury's *Fahrenheit 451*, the False Utopia is a prison disguised as an ideal world. In this section of the book you'll find all you need to regain your free will and start the revolution.

NEO-MEDIEVALISM: After the fall of civilization you'll need to improvise a lot. This section will help you redefine your persona, survive in all climates, and kick some serious ass.

THE ADVANCED TECHNOLOGICAL DYSTOPIA: Technology has run rampant, all corporations have merged into one, and there are aliens jumping out of people's chests at dinner. You're going to need some help.

And finally, **APOCALYPSE THEN: TIPS FOR SAVING THE WORLD:** Giant insects, Orson Welles, whatever.

Keep in mind that with careful study, calculated preparation, and a positive attitude . . . you'll probably still die. But just in case you don't, I offer you the *Field Guide to the Apocalypse.* As you can see, this information couldn't have come at a better time.

In order to help you get started, take the following quiz to determine which apocalypse you're likely headed for. Don't worry. It's not like that sorting-hat thing from Harry Potter—nothing permanent or life altering. Good luck, soldier. I'll see you in the bunker.

take me to
my leader: a quiz

1 **When dining out, you are more likely to order:**

a. Taco Bell

b. Sushi

c. You'll just eat someone's leftovers

2 **Your dream car is:**

a. K.I.T.T. from *Knight Rider*

b. A Geo Metro

c. A 1974 Ford Falcon

3 **You are more likely to need legal advice at:**

a. The Interrogation

b. The Cryochamber

c. The Monkey House

4 **Your lawyer is:**

a. Charged with the same offense

b. A computer

c. The Man in the Yellow Hat

5 **Your significant other disappears without a trace.
You assume:**

a. S/he turned thirty

b. S/he's one of "them" now

c. S/he's taken the cat and left for Alpha Centauri

6　At night you sleep with:

　　a. Pharmacological assistance
　　b. A gun
　　c. Whomever will have you

7　Choose one:

　　a. Desert
　　b. Jungle
　　c. Suburbia

8　Your friends are having a shindig in your honor. It is most likely a:

　　a. Funeral
　　b. Bonfire
　　c. LAN party

9　The light at the end of the tunnel is:

　　a. A train
　　b. The entrance to the mine shaft
　　c. The secret police

10　Your favorite place to shop is:

　　a. IKEA
　　b. Victory Auto Wreckers
　　c. eBay

11 Your drink of choice is:

a. Grain alcohol

b. Sake

c. vitaminwater

12 The glass is:

a. Broken

b. Half full

c. There is no glass

SCORE YOURSELF

1. a: 1, b: 3, c: 2	5. a: 1, b: 2, c: 3	9. a: 3, b: 2, c: 1
2. a: 3, b: 1, c: 2	6. a: 1, b: 2, c: 3	10. a: 1, b: 2, c: 3
3. a: 1, b: 3, c: 2	7. a: 2, b: 3, c: 1	11. a: 2, b: 3, c: 1
4. a: 1, b: 3, c: 2	8. a: 1, b: 2, c: 3	12. a: 2, b: 1, c: 3

If you scored:

12-19: You're headed for the False Utopia. Please discontinue the use of all mind-altering medications and refrain from drinking the tap water until you begin to regain free will. Then turn to Part I, on page 1, and stay away from your television.

20-27: Neo-Medievalism, here you come! You're self-reliant almost to the point of psychosis. Grab your leather jacket and turn to Part II on page 31. Don't forget the sawed-off shotgun. You'll need it.

28-36: Advanced Technological Dystopia. You're comfy with technology, and that's great! That'll be handy once the machines rise. Grab a machete and a laptop and dive into the urban technological jungle by turning to Part III on page 127.

PART I: the false utopia

the false utopia

The year was 2081 and everyone was finally equal.
—KURT VONNEGUT JR., "HARRISON BERGERON"

THE MIDDLE OF THE TWENTY-FIRST CENTURY IS DRAWING NEAR.
Government has swallowed up most of the corporations. Genetic research is advancing at an astounding rate. It is now possible to accomplish with science what nature could not. The population is carefully controlled for optimum efficiency. Humanity is approaching perfection. There is no violence, no crime—no hate. Children obey their parents, get to school on time, and always do their homework. There is never any MSG in Chinese food. Ever.

PROFILE

EXPECTED TIME FRAME: 2030–?

TYPE OF GOVERNMENT: Police State

MAIN INDUSTRIES: Government, Pharmaceuticals, Genetics

LAW ENFORCEMENT: Military Police

CORRECTIONS: Euthanasia

ESTIMATED HUMAN POPULATION: 2–3 billion

what is it?

The False Utopia is a society that appears perfect. Life's most vexing problems have been solved: inequality, crime, aging, poverty, depression. . . . Unfortunately, nothing comes without a cost, and in the case of the False Utopia, that cost is carefully concealed from the citizens . . . only to be discovered just as they're hitting the meat grinder. *Don't let this happen to you!*

Despite all the subterfuge involved, there are still reliable ways of assessing your situation. Study the following chapters carefully and you may be able to make your escape—*before* it's too late.

TEN SIGNS THAT YOU MAY BE LIVING IN A FALSE UTOPIA

10 There are no old people. Life expectancy should hover around eighty to eighty-five years. So if you are having trouble finding anyone over thirty, there is cause for alarm.

9 Lack of education. If your knowledge of history is reminiscent of *Xena: Warrior Princess,* the outlook is not good.

8 Compulsory attendance and/or genetic testing. Ask yourself: *What if I didn't go this week?* If the answer involves pit bulls or Jude Law's urine, the time to act is now.

7 Everyone wears the same creepy, unflattering outfits. If spandex or "tunics" are involved, go ahead and score this one double.

6   You don't know where the food comes from. It is imperative that you find out immediately, especially if you also don't know what the food *is*.

5   Everyone says the same dippy catchphrase when entering or leaving a conversation. Examples include: "Be well," "Go carefully," and "Heil" anybody.

4   Required "Medicine." If you stop taking it, do the pit bulls come back?

3   Sex is a crime.

2   The crime rate is "zero."

1   They're trying to arrest you for reading this.

THE VERDICT: If any of these scenarios sound familiar, get out now! Your society is a prison hellhole. Any moment now you could be made into sausage and served to Charlton Heston. What if you don't want to go? Well, don't blame me if your thirtieth birthday party is at the Oscar Mayer plant. I tried to warn you. For the rest of you, come with me if you want to live.

culture, sex, and fashion in the false utopia

"You mean . . . Fluid Transfer?"
—LENINA HUXLEY (SANDRA BULLOCK), *DEMOLITION MAN*

religious beliefs

A wide variety of religions and philosophies will appeal to people in a False Utopia, but they'll share some common characteristics:

- Disdain for the uncivilized past

- Confidence in the new order

- Complicated rituals

- Authority figures who are not to be questioned

TIP: If there is one particular ritual that people never come back from, politely pass. If anyone asks you to get on a carousel, for example, don't do it.

mental health

The concept of mental health is radically different in a False Utopia. Emotions are considered unhealthy and often suppressed with medication. "A gram is better than a damn," goes one popular saying. In some societies medication to eliminate emotions will be compulsory.

sex and reproduction

Sexual contact may be discouraged or even outlawed. Virtual-reality sex may become the only acceptable alternative. Most likely, reproduction will be carefully monitored by the government to prevent overpopulation. Genetic screening and engineering will allow prospective parents to tailor-make their progeny based on their own genetic information.

In some cases reproduction will be handled solely by the government, which will use selective breeding and subliminal messaging to create a caste system.

recreation

Television will most likely be the recreational activity of choice in the False Utopia. Here there is an inverse relationship between personal freedom and television size. The bigger the TV, the less freedom that is afforded the individual. Short, easily digested programs will dominate the broadcasting schedule. The television will likely broadcast both ways and not have an off switch. The television is there to keep you company—and in the False Utopia to prefer to be alone is to be considered unhealthy or mentally unstable. Solitary activities like reading and studying are discouraged and replaced by group projects and lectures.

fashion

Fashion in the False Utopia will be directly tied to social status. You are what you wear, so to speak. You wear either: (1) dorky-ass lounging wear or (2) a uniform. That's pretty much it, fashion-wise.

LOUNGING WEAR: Lounging wear is really the only way to describe the clothes people will be wearing in the False Utopia. Often the style is pseudo-Japanese, but not as cool. Here are some necessary items for the "Utopian Lounge Look":

- *Tailored Robes:* These should be in a variety of muted colors. Beige is very popular. You should look like either a samurai on holiday or a minister of some sort.

- *Shoes That Match:* Everything matches in the future.

- *Hats That Look Like the Vince Lombardi Trophy:* Why this is necessary, I have no idea.

- *No Pockets:* In the future we will not need pockets; we'll all be microchipped like cats.

- *Tunics and Tights:* This is a popular option for societies where there are no old, fat people.

> **TIP:** If your outfit is color coded to your age, watch out. If your name also ends with a number (e.g., Julia 6, Dilbert 9, Heloise 3), just start running now.

UNIFORMS: Uniforms in the False Utopia will be streamlined and intimidating. Here are the necessary items for your uniform:

- **The Mock Turtleneck:** This is essential, really. Nothing says badass like a mock turtleneck. A really tight mock turtleneck.

- **The Elementary School Safety Patrol Belt:** Because accidents happen even in a utopian society. You may cross.

- **Big Tall Shiny Boots:** For extra scare factor.

- **Nightstick:** For zapping people who swear or wear jeans.

- **Beret:** Should be roguishly tilted for maximum effect.

- **Mirrored Sunglasses:** So you can pull off the whole *Cool Hand Luke* look.

how to get off mind-controlling drugs

"It's incredibly obvious, isn't it?
A foreign substance is introduced into our
precious bodily fluids without the knowledge
of the individual—certainly without any choice."

—GENERAL JACK D. RIPPER (STERLING HAYDEN),
DR. STRANGELOVE; OR, HOW I LEARNED TO
STOP WORRYING AND LOVE THE BOMB

A government drugging its citizens into complacency is one of the most insidious possibilities you may face in the post-apocalyptic world. Like General Ripper, you could decide to order the 183rd Bomb Wing to attack its targets inside Russia; but unless you're one of a very small number of individuals, you will probably not have this kind of authority. Besides, even if you could order a nuclear attack, it hardly seems fair to the Russians.

DISCLAIMER: Thinking that someone is trying to control your mind is a symptom of some pretty heinous mental disorders that you should probably rule out before attempting anything in this book. Thanks.

In the case of a massive mind-control conspiracy, it is always a good policy to help yourself before you try to help others[1]—just like with the oxygen mask on an airplane. Here are some steps for doing just that:

1　Discontinue any medications labeled MIND CONTROL PILLS, MK-ULTRA, HAPPY VITAMINS, or SOMA.

2　Drink only grain alcohol and rainwater. Fluoride may help your teeth, but is that *all* that's coming out of your tap? Also, who is bottling that water? Do you trust them?

3　Watch for signs of burgeoning free will. These may include (but are not limited to): increased libido; happiness; curiosity; craving for chocolate, beer, or pizza; opinions; laziness; selfishness; ennui; decrease in suggestibility; reformation of values; and the desire to sit around in your shorts and watch *The Price Is Right*.[2]

4　If you are experiencing no signs of free will, check your body for timed-release drug patches or scars from surgery that you don't remember. Take steps as necessary.

5　Use free will wisely. On the surface you must appear to conform—or risk dire consequences. Conceal your newly found free will from others. There may be people close to you who have been trained to detect and report it. Keep your own counsel until such time as you are able to free others.

[1] Or start World War III.

[2] *The Price Is Right* will still be on television even after society has done away with currency and the show is hosted by Bob Barker's head in a jar.

how to conceal free will

Ticket Agent: "What's the matter with your eyes?"
Roger Thornhill: "They're sensitive to questions."

—*NORTH BY NORTHWEST*

ow that you've freed yourself from the effects of mind control, it's time to start thinking about your future. Free will is a dangerous commodity in the False Utopia. Once you've regained yours, you'll need to disguise it or else run the risk of being "recycled" and served at Yankee Stadium.[3] This won't be easy. You will be living outside the law in a society that does not tolerate diversity. *Start planning your escape now.* You won't be able to keep up the charade for very long. Keep a low profile.

1   Make no changes in your routine. Be cool. Act natural.[4]
If you have a brainwashed spouse, attempt to free him or her only if you are certain that you will be successful. You might want to take into account the fact that when you are not on medication, you might not like each other. Keep dramatic speeches about human dignity and the intrinsic value of life to a minimum at this stage.

---

[3] In the future all stadiums will be Yankee Stadium.
[4] Or unnatural. Whatever.

2 Carefully hide all reading materials and other contraband. Keep them somewhere that cannot be directly linked to you. Wear gloves and take steps to prevent the transfer of DNA.

GOOD HIDING PLACES

- Under the left-field bleachers

- Under that loose floorboard in the closet at work

- Vents and ducts in other people's homes [5]

- Abandoned vehicles and buildings—make sure they are easily accessible

---

[5] Consider this an opportunity to flex your newfound emotions and experiment with passive aggression.

BAD HIDING PLACES

- Under the bed

- In the glove box

- In your bra[6]

- "In plain sight"—you aren't Edgar Allan Poe

- In the way, way, waaaay back of the closet

- In the freezer behind the microwave tacos

3. Plan your escape. You will not be able to keep up pretenses for very long. Within one to two weeks, you will begin to arouse suspicion in your friends and colleagues. Here are some tips for escaping alive:

- Locate other members of the resistance and join them. They will be more receptive of you if you possess a skill or access to critical information. If you hold a strategic position, you may be enlisted as a spy or as a diversion. These roles involve additional risk—accept only if the reward[7] outweighs the danger to your person.

- Stockpile weapons and learn to use them. You will need them in the third act.

- Bring ample supplies. Remember when you packed a bag and ran away from home—only to go to the park two blocks away, eat your Lunchables, and run back home? You can't do

[6] Just because it worked at the Radiohead concert does not mean it will still work.
[7] Single-handedly saving the world, the downfall of the Evil Empire, destroying the Death Star, etc.

that this time. Bring at least a week's worth of supplies. And don't forget lightweight luxury items to barter with. If items are rationed, stockpile them inconspicuously.

- Don't attract attention to yourself. Make sure all your papers are in order. Obtain false ones if necessary. Do everything possible to avoid standing out in the crowd. Above all, be confident. It takes courage to contradict a confident person. Bank on the weakness of others. Always look like you know what you are doing and have every right to do it.

some final tips for appearing brainwashed

- Stare straight ahead a lot. Try not to move your eyes around unless you need to look at something. If you see a person being horribly murdered, just cock your head quizzically and do nothing. Remember, hands at your sides—you're brainwashed, not sleepwalking.

- Keep your appearance up. No running out to Denny's at three a.m. in your tracksuit pants and that No Fear T-shirt you thought was so funny in junior high.

- Don't fidget or look nervous. Remember, the mindless have nothing to worry about. Remain enthusiastic and respond normally to propaganda. If your boss calls you in for a "little talk," reaffirm your patriotism and devotion to the cause.

- Do not under any circumstances ask well-meaning questions.

how to recognize
a dream world

> Ever drifting down the stream—
> Lingering in the golden gleam—
> Life, what is it but a dream?
> —LEWIS CARROLL, EPILOGUE TO
> *THROUGH THE LOOKING GLASS*

A dream world is a subset of the False Utopia. It's a more personal apocalypse, one that can exist entirely in your own head. You might even be plugged into a machine or living in someone else's dream. You really can't be sure.

To help you get a grip on what you may be dealing with, here is a list of common symptoms of a false reality:

1. There are white rabbits that mutter a lot. Actually, any cryptic reference to a white rabbit is cause for concern.

2. You experience a dramatic increase in confusing symbolism. For example, there are high-wheeled bicycles, umbrellas, and British people wearing silly hats for no apparent reason.

3. Everything is strange and different, but everyone acts as if nothing out of the ordinary has happened.

4   You wake up in a strange bathroom with amnesia and/or a dead person.

5   Men in suits and sunglasses are following you, calling you "Mr. Anderson" in what appears to be a totally hopeless attempt at an American accent.

6   People refer to geographic features or places generically and as if there were only one of them (e.g., "The Mountains," "The Village," "The Highway").

7   There is an ambiguous authority figure with a catchy name: "The Wizard," "Number One," "The Architect," "The Queen of Hearts,"[8] and so on.

8   You're in a town surrounded by some woods with mythical creatures[9] in it, or there is some other sort of barrier or guardian keeping you from getting too far away.

9   You get everything you've ever wanted all at once.

10   You are involved in wildly popular and critically acclaimed weekly episodic adventures in which you always seem to end up in exactly the same state in which you started, but something strange, life altering, and seemingly irreversible has happened.

[8] "The Lord of the Dance"?
[9] Adrian Brody is not a mythical creature.

determining if
you are dreaming

There's no way to be 100 percent certain that you are awake. However, there are some tricks that you can try:

- Try reading something. If you are dreaming, you will probably not be able to read. The words should be all mixed up and sdfjw readcnd weryasdh twer. Fdfeinefds. I dfeb the dfbtudfnh, wernngh gud.

- Turn the lights on. If nothing happens, you may be dreaming. Or you may need to run to the hardware store.

- Look at your watch. Concentrate on making the numbers change. If they do, you're probably dreaming. Also, the time might not make sense. There is no twenty-five o'clock, even in Europe. If your watch says something like this, you are dreaming.

- Look at the phone. Try to make it ring. If it does, you are probably dreaming.[10]

Once you've determined that you are no longer in touch with reality, you have several options. You *could* try to wake yourself up. The problem with this is, unless you know what you will find, you might be better off staying put and learning to control your dream world. Lucid dreaming can be very rewarding. You could learn to fly, turn all the cats pink, and beat up that bully from second grade—who knows?

---

[10] You also might want to consider the possibility that you are just the lamest X-Man ever.

I personally would try to find Bruce Willis, but the possibilities are endless. Waking up might mean that you have to eat gross white porridge stuff and dress like you're from Tatooine. On the plus side, you may get to hang out with Joe Pantoliano, until he tries to kill you. Or you could wind up in Kansas. You really can't be sure.

what to do if you might be trapped in a dream and don't know it

See, this is bad. There is just no way to tell if you are dreaming. If you are trapped in a dream, chances are that someone will eventually come and try to wake you up by *giving you a pill*. What you need to do is figure out whether or not they are really just trying to kill you. In *Total Recall,* Sharon Stone's character was actually trying to kill Arnold's character, or more likely, she was trying to drug him so the bad guys could mess with his brain. Arnie figured this out because the "doctor" she brought along was sweating and nervous. Therefore, he did not take the pill, which was probably going to be really bad for him. On the other hand, in *The Matrix,* Laurence Fishburne's character *was* telling the truth, and he made a very convincing argument in those awkwardly metered sentences of his. Laurence Fishburne seems really trustworthy. He played Othello. Sharon Stone is, like, totally creepy and kills people with ice picks while smoking and not wearing underwear. You can compare and contrast these two scenes and decide whether or not the person offering you the pill is more like Sharon Stone or Laurence Fishburne. The following quiz may help you, but ultimately, the decision is up to you.

the stone/fishburne hypothesis diagnostic test

NOTE: "The subject" refers to the person offering you the pill. "You" refers to you.

1 How recently has the subject kicked your ass?

a. Never
b. This morning

2 Do you feel that the subject is more or less likely to wear spandex while kicking your ass?

a. Less
b. More

3 Is the subject patronizing and cryptic?

a. Yes
b. No, the subject is cloying and sympathetic

4 Is the subject wearing sunglasses?

a. Yes, and we're inside and it's night
b. No

5 Have you seen the subject naked?

a. Yes, accidentally
b. Yes, accidentally on purpose

If you chose mostly A's: You're probably awake. Kick the subject's ass.

If you chose mostly B's: You're trapped in a dream world. Look on the bright side: At least you have the sunglasses to look forward to.

waking up

The best way to wake up is to distance yourself from what is going on in the dream. One popular method is to go to sleep *within the dream*. Often this will cause you to wake up. Be careful, however, as you may cause yourself to only *think* that you're waking up, when really you're just dreaming that you've woken up, and in fact you are still dreaming. Oh, dear. I've gone cross-eyed.

how to not die in your dreams

It's like Captain Kirk[11] said: "If we do not allow ourselves to believe the bullets are real, they cannot kill us." You'll notice it was Captain Kirk who said that and not T. J. Hooker.

The idea of death being caused by dying in your dreams got really popular in the 1980s and then mutated and became virtual-reality death, as in *The Matrix* and "Your mind makes it real" and so forth. The whole thing sounds pretty fishy to me, but I suppose it's best to not die in your dreams if at all possible. Not only is it unpleasant to die violently at the hands of some weirdo with knives for fingers, it's hard for your parents to explain to the police.

[11] William Shatner kicks ass.

Here are some tips for not dying in your dreams:

- Don't walk slowly along long hallways looking apprehensively left and right. You're dreaming. Run around screaming and try to wake yourself up.

- At the first sign of a red-and-black-striped shirt, get the fuck out of there.

- Don't go into other people's dreams and try to kill them. By the third act someone will be a total dream ninja and give you a taste of your own medicine.

- Don't sneak into other people's sexy dreams about you. It's just rude.

- If you fall off something, wake up before you hit the ground. Or, conversely, imagine real hard that there is a big trampoline down there.

how to not wake up

Maybe your dream world rules? I mean, it could happen—right? Who am I to say that your dream world is full of people with bad fashion sense, bent on torturing you with endless repetition, assigning you a number, trying everything they can to break you down mentally, and forcing you to succumb to their will? Wait, am I talking about *The Prisoner* or your mall job? Think about it.

In any case, if you actually like your dream world and wish to continue dreaming, experts on lucid dreaming suggest that you try spinning with your arms out. They have no idea why this works, and neither do I.

my food is people

"It's people! Soylent Green
is made out of people!"
—ROBERT THORN (CHARLTON HESTON),
SOYLENT GREEN

That's right, folks: *Soylent Green is people.*

Glad we got that out of the way.

If you are living in a society where the population has gotten totally out of control and the resultant food shortage is being miraculously solved by an evil corporation, you might want to pay close attention to this chapter.

Here are some things to watch out for—some really *obvious* signs that your food is people:

- There is a food shortage caused by overpopulation.

- People are in queues waiting for oddly colored food substances made from "high-energy vegetable concentrates." Mmm. Tasty.

- One of these oddly colored food types is wildly more popular than the others.

- Riot control involves bulldozers that harvest—er, I mean *arrest*—unruly citizens.

- People are encouraged to commit suicide, but no one really knows what they do with the bodies.

Obviously, if your food is people, someone should figure it out pretty quickly and put a stop to it. But let's wait just one moment. Supposedly, the most nutritious foods are the ones most closely resembling your own constitution—so Soylent Green might not be such a bad idea after all. The people sure seem to like it, the corporations are making a bundle, and what's good for Soylent Enterprises is good for the country. . . .

Speaking of corporations, have you ever thought about what's in the food you eat? Here's how to be certain that sausage isn't a former member of the Taliban or something:

1   Go to where they're killing people.

2   Watch for someone you know. When you find someone . . .

3   Pay attention to what room they go in.

4   Wait for them to die.

5   Follow the body.

You have to be careful, especially during the last step. Odds are that Soylent Corporation won't want the news getting out that instead of "plankton," they're actually serving Pete from apartment 2A.

One more thing: You'll notice that the bodies weren't actually butchered. They were just loaded on a conveyor belt and dropped into a tank. This seems like a really bad idea. Bodies have things like hair and teeth and digestive tracts. Also worth noting is that in The Matrix the humans were also being fed liquefied people, but it was pink. Soylent Pink is people!

how to not be replaced by a robot

"What's the going price for
a stay-in-the-kitchen wife with
big boobs and no demands? . . .
And what happens to the real ones?
The incinerator? Stepford Pond?"
—IRA LEVIN, *THE STEPFORD WIVES*

The first thing you're going to want to do in this situation is make sure someone is actually trying to replace you with a robot. It would be a shame to stab a perfectly nice man in the neck with a big-ass Michael Myers knife just for asking you to stop leaving your coffee mugs in the living room.

Here are the symptoms of a partner who is scheming to upgrade your hardware:

- Hangs out in clubs you can't join due to lack of organic phallus

- Likes Connecticut

- Plays golf

- Quite obviously is anticipating something

- Critical of your career and hobbies

- Change in sex drive

- Friends with Disney animatronics expert

If your partner is exhibiting some or all of these symptoms, you may want to start evaluating your surroundings.

Have you:

- Recently moved to a small, affluent town?

- Noticed anything odd about the women there?

- Felt the need to subscribe to *Martha Stewart Living*?

- Noticed that your ice cubes aren't as clear as they could be? Or that the thread count of your linens is just not up to par?

- Recently started using phrases like *not up to par*?

> **TIP:** Emergency Warning Signs: If anyone comes to your house to record your voice for a "personal project," don't do it. They are making a robot of you. Evacuate immediately. Also, if your former best friend offers to cut herself to prove she's not a robot, let her do it from across the room.

At this point you will have determined whether or not you are, in fact, in danger of being replaced. If you need to gather more evidence, do so discreetly. The sooner they are onto you, the sooner they will schedule your replacement.

how to not be replaced

STEP 1: Do not allow yourself to be alone with your partner. Sneak out the back door, climb out a window—whatever it takes.

STEP 2: Do not trust anyone who is holding a knife. Grab the car keys and get out of town. File for divorce.

STEP 3: If attacked during your escape, stab the attacker repeatedly with a large kitchen knife. Aim for the neck.

PART II: the neo-medieval world

the neo-medieval world

It can be argued that the emergence of any intelligent species co-opting a planet's resources in the service of advanced technology and agriculture will necessarily cause a planetary mass extinction.

—PETER D. WARD AND DONALD BROWNLEE,
RARE EARTH: WHY COMPLEX LIFE IS UNCOMMON IN THE UNIVERSE

"Human sacrifice; dogs and cats—living together . . . mass hysteria!"

—PETER VENKMAN (BILL MURRAY), *GHOSTBUSTERS*

PROFILE

EXPECTED TIME FRAME: 2014–?

TYPE OF GOVERNMENT: Anarchy

MAIN INDUSTRIES: Looting, Bounty Hunting

LAW ENFORCEMENT: Not Applicable

CORRECTIONS: Exile, Hand-to-Hand Combat

ESTIMATED HUMAN POPULATION: Unknown

LIFE AS WE KNOW IT IS OVER. There is no government, no electricity, no running water. All corporations have ceased to exist. Most of the human population has perished for one reason or another. You are one of the "lucky ones." You're still here. The precious few survivors get by on what they can scavenge from the ruins of a once-mighty civilization. Life basically sucks, but at least you no longer have to worry about parking tickets.

what is it?

The Neo-Medieval World is a harsh place to live in. Civilization has fallen and it has fallen hard. The system has broken down. To thrive in the postapocalyptic landscape will require a variety of survival skills for a variety of potential apocalypses. You must be ready for anything. In the event of another ice age, desert survival skills won't do you very much good.

Just to cheer you up, here is a brief overview of possible (and in some cases probable) apocalypses and the theories behind them:

supervolcano

Yellowstone Park is one giant supervolcano. It's 40,000 years overdue to explode with 2,000 times the force of Mount Saint Helens. It will expel enough lava to cover most of the continental United States. Most likely, the ash will send the planet into nuclear winter, killing all life above ground.

THE BAD NEWS: This volcano *will* erupt eventually; in fact, it's already showing signs of life. Parts of the park have been shut down because the ground is simply too hot to walk on. Records show that the level of the rock has swelled almost one meter in eighty years. It will erupt soon. We just don't know when.

meteor strike

Everyone's heard about how a meteorite hit the planet and killed all the dinosaurs. But could the same thing happen again? Sure. Why the hell not? This is the most common and likely of the disaster scenarios.

To be fair, there *are* several factors that make meteor strikes on the order of magnitude needed to extinguish life on the planet rather rare events. First of all, the relative close proximity of a huge-ass planet like Jupiter is actually not only fortunate, but necessary. Jupiter's huge gravitational pull sucks away pesky things like comets and large hunks of rock, leaving Earth relatively unperturbed. Secondly, our moon makes a pretty decent target for a lot of space junk, as you can tell just by looking at it. And thirdly, the friction caused by our atmosphere burns away whatever tries to enter it. So we have a lot going for us, planetarily speaking. In fact, if we didn't, we wouldn't be here at all. Every few thousand years or so, a great bleeding hunk of something or other would smash into the planet and kill everything on it. Thanks to our atmosphere and friendly planetary neighbors, this doesn't happen. And yet, the odd extinction by meteorite does occur. *C'est la vie.*

A meteorite does not have to cause extinction, however. Meteors are perfectly capable of taking out cities, causing mega-tsunamis, wiping out continents, or just ruining Bob's new 'Vette. It all depends. Scientists, having realized that it would, like, totally suck if a huge meteor hit the planet, have begun tracking what they call Near Earth Objects, or NEOs. They think they've just about found them all, and at least one of them is special.

THE BAD NEWS: One of these NEOs has a 930,009 to 1 chance of hitting Earth in the year 2014. Cosmologically speaking, that's practically a sure thing. Now, this particular meteor will probably not hit the planet, and as it gets closer scientists will be able to better calculate how much it will miss by. Apparently, *this sort of thing happens all the time*—and there have been much closer misses than this one. That's actually meant to be comforting. If you're the gambling sort, there is a bookie in the UK who is taking bets that this meteor will strike the planet. He astutely notes that should you win, he will probably not have to pay you anyway.

climate change

Better known as *global warming*, climate change is the single greatest threat facing our civilization's future. While the supervolcano and meteor strike scenarios *will* eventually happen, there's always the chance that we'll either have the technology to prevent them or we'll already be extinct by the time they get around to happening. *Why would we be extinct?* To put it bluntly: climate change. It turns out that our friendly little planet has a mean streak. Climate change happens *rapidly*—far more rapidly that we originally thought. Instead of taking thousands of years, a severe bout of climate change can take less than a decade, and the damage is irreversible. For example, there have been five major extinctions in Earth's history. The worst one was caused by global warming. Let's take a look at what happens to the planet during a period of climate change.

First, an increase in carbon dioxide (CO_2) gas causes the atmosphere to act like a blanket, trapping heat that would otherwise escape into space. CO_2 gas comes from various sources, but the most important one is from the burning of fossil fuels. When we burn fossil fuels, we release CO_2 that was formerly stored in the ground. It took the planet millions of years to store up enough CO_2 to provide us with the balmy and perfectly balanced atmosphere we are currently enjoying. By burning fossil fuels, we are tampering with this balance.

When the planet gets warmer, a bunch of stuff happens:

- The polar ice caps melt (already in progress).

- The sea level rises (up to fifty-five meters).

- Important ocean currents shut down.

The ice caps represent approximately 50 percent of the world's supply of freshwater. As the ice forms it leaves behind extremely salty seawater. This denser, heavier water sinks to the bottom of the ocean, reemerging a millennium later as the Gulf Stream or "Conveyor" that supplies Europe and the rest of the Northern Hemisphere with its relatively temperate climate. Without this current, Europe would really suck. It would be cold and shitty all the time. This whole process is called *thermohaline circulation*.

THE BAD NEWS: So what does this all mean? So the planet gets warmer and Europe gets colder? What is the big deal?

Well, trapped in the permafrost there are huge—really, really huge— reservoirs of methane gas. Methane gas is about twice as effective as CO_2 at retaining heat, which means that we *really* don't want methane in the atmosphere. So let's just go through what will happen if global warming continues:

- The polar ice caps melt rapidly. New ice fails to form, shutting down the current that goes from the tropics to the North Atlantic.

- Europe cools down. The equator superheats, due to a lack of cold water from the north.

- The rain forests die from too much heat. As they rot they release huge amounts of CO_2 into the atmosphere. Now the planet's getting really hot.

- The huge reservoirs of methane gas trapped in the frozen layers of the planet melt and are released. This sends global warming out of control.

Once the planet has warmed enough to release the methane gas, we will have a situation on our hands. The worst extinction in our planet's history was caused by this very same scenario. The result? Ninety-five percent of all species became extinct, making it by far the worst extinction that the planet has faced. No meteors, no nuclear war, nothing at all except a temperature shift. *And how much global warming was enough to trigger the most severe extinction in planetary history?* A modest six degrees Celsius.

And here we are, already well on our way. But what would really happen? Well, after the rain forests died, the planet would be hard-pressed to provide enough oxygen for everyone to breathe. Evaporation would increase, turning most of North America into something not unlike the Sahara Desert. Without this key food-producing region, millions worldwide would starve. Nations would build up nuclear arms to protect a dwindling supply of food and freshwater. Coastal cities would be wiped out by rising sea levels, and much marine life would be killed by the increase in ocean temperature. Eventually, most living things would starve, be eaten, or be killed. The possibility of this happening is so real and so immediate that the Pentagon has proclaimed climate change a matter of national security and commissioned a report that predicted these events could transpire as soon as 2030.

ice age

Ice ages come around roughly every 100,000 years and are tied to little wobbles in Earth's orbit. It seems as if there's one for sending us into an ice age and another one for getting us back out. But it's not so simple. There also appears to be a connection between the CO_2 content in the atmosphere and the periods of glaciation. Basically, an ice age begins with a little cooling. This can be caused by a planetary wobble or *maybe* the shutdown of thermohaline circulation (remember?) in concert with a little-known phenomenon known as *global dimming*. Stay with me here.

GLOBAL DIMMING: *Global dimming* is the term used to describe the fact that each year we are receiving less and less sunlight on the ground. The effect is so pronounced that between 1950 and 1980 there was a 10 percent overall decrease in solar radiation. Scientists have recently confirmed an approximate 3 percent decrease in sunlight per decade. This troubling effect explains why evaporation, rather than going up as would be expected during a period of global warming, is actually going down.

What does this mean? Since the sun is putting out the same (if not more) radiation, something must have happened to the atmosphere to prevent sunlight from hitting the ground. The current popular guess is that particles from industry, smoke, smog, and other pollutants are reflecting solar radiation in the visible and infrared part of the spectrum (UV radiation is not affected). Currently, the effect is actually *countering* that of global warming—helping the atmosphere act more like a dark wet blanket than a clear plastic sheet.

THE BAD NEWS: Ice ages are thought to happen when a chain reaction leads to more and more ice being formed at the poles. Ice reflects more sunlight than the dark ground or even the ocean. This causes heat to be shot back into space, cooling the planet and leading to the formation of more ice. Again this new ice is shinier than what it once covered, and the effect progresses until nearly the entire Northern Hemisphere is covered with 1,000-meter-thick glaciers. The amount of light absorbed/reflected by the planet is known as its *albedo*. All that is needed to begin the process is sufficient cooling in the Northern Hemisphere. A little warming—enough to halt the formation of new ice and shut down the Gulf Stream—could paradoxically provide enough *cooling* to get an ice age started prematurely. Combine this with the already significant decrease in sunlight caused by global dimming and you could have a serious problem on your hands. Or more specifically, a 1,000-meter-thick problem providing us with icebergs as far south as Portugal. Or not. It's all theoretical.

pandemic

If you ask around, few people will be able to name the largest pandemic in human history. By largest, I mean the most people dead in the shortest amount of time from one disease. By all accounts that would be the Influenza Pandemic of 1918. In one year's time influenza killed anywhere from twenty to forty million (yes, million) people worldwide. These numbers are hard to imagine in a world where we issue travel warnings and wear surgical masks for epidemics that kill less than 800 people. The SARS epidemic, which, according to the World Health Organization, killed 774 people worldwide, is recognized and feared, while the humble fact that regular old influenza kills 36,000 Americans every year lies in relative obscurity. And that's when there's an ample amount of the vaccine.

The Influenza Pandemic of 1918 killed ten times as many Americans as did World War I, and even some of those war casualties were actually from influenza and not from the enemy. This was not just the ordinary flu. It was incredibly infectious and attacked its hosts quickly, filling their lungs with fluid and suffocating them. Morgues had stacks of bodies waiting to be buried, and the morticians simply refused to work, leaving the families of the dead to bury their own. Often the victims would turn blue as they died, blood running from their noses and ears.

But of course the pandemic was helped along by the war, by casual reassurances from a government that did nothing, and by the lack of medical knowledge and effective vaccines. Surely this could not happen today. Right?

THE BAD NEWS: Recent research conducted on the lung tissue of an influenza victim frozen in the Arctic has confirmed that the Influenza Pandemic of 1918 was caused by mutated bird flu. Why is this important? Bird flu is different from human influenza in that it has different signature substances. Basically, a human immune system understands what a human influenza virus is like. Because the influenza virus mutates frequently, you can never really achieve total immunity—but your body basically knows what it is dealing with. When a person contracts bird flu, the body is confused. It's not prepared. It doesn't know what to do. Your body has no defense. Thankfully, although humans do sometimes contract bird flu, it cannot be passed from human to human. Or can it?

If a person contracts bird flu *and* human influenza at the same time, there could be trouble. The viruses could mix RNA and produce a hybrid— one with the infectious nature of human influenza, but one that the immune system fails to recognize. It's happened before. What you will have is the Influenza Pandemic of 1918. Twenty to forty million people dead. The virus infected one fifth of the world's population and around one third of America. It also did not attack the very young and the very old, the way that regular influenza does. This virus's highest mortality rate was among those twenty to forty years of age.

gamma ray burst

When a large star exhausts all of its fuel, it begins collapsing into itself. The dying star gets hotter and hotter until it eventually causes a gigantic explosion known as a *supernova*. Along with jettisoning huge amounts of matter and energy, a supernova generates what is called a *gamma ray burst*.

This innocuous-sounding phenomenon could be responsible for one of the mass extinctions here on Earth. A new theory suggests that a supernova within the proximity of 1,000 light-years once produced a gamma ray burst that fried Earth's ozone layer, removing its protection from the harmful rays of the sun. More recently (i.e., 20,000 years ago), a star undergoing some sort of reaction let loose a burst of gamma rays that arrived in 1998. The burst took out some satellites and got within thirty miles of the surface of Earth before our lovely atmosphere took care of it. Had the star been closer, we might not have been so lucky.

THE BAD NEWS: Another supernova could come at any time. There is absolutely no way to avoid it or predict it because gamma rays travel at the speed of light. We literally wouldn't see it coming until it was already here. The ozone layer would burn off, the sky would turn brown, and plant and animal life would begin to die. Thankfully, according to predictions based on the occurrence of supernovas in our galactic neighborhood, the likely frequency of a gamma ray burst hitting Earth is about once every 700 million years.[12] Sweet.

nuclear war

The cold war is over, but still, you never know. They nuke us, we nuke them back . . . pretty soon the whole atmosphere is full of soot and ash, and we've got nuclear winter.

---

[12] It should be noted that there seems to be quite a bit of dispute about the likelihood of this happening. Some scientists think that we're totally doomed and that there are bursts on the way now. There have even been theories about possible explosions in deep space that are powerful enough to destroy the fabric of space and time. Yikes.

THE BAD NEWS: There are significantly more nuclear powers today than there were fifty years ago, and some of them are potentially psycho. Not naming any names,

biblical apocalypse

Some "facts" about the biblical apocalypse:

1   There is something called "the Rapture," where all the true believers will be summoned up to heaven. This may or may not happen before the frogs fall from the sky, depending on who is indoctrinating you.

2   All the really scary stuff happens—horsemen, seas boiling, bloody moon, and all that—before the Second Coming of Jesus. After that there is a thousand-year reign of peace, which doesn't sound so bad, actually.

3   The Four Horsemen of the Apocalypse are Famine, Pestilence, Death, and Ringo. No, I'm sorry, that was an obvious joke. There are actually only three: Wacko, Yacko, and Death. No, that's not it either. I don't know. I bet Stephen Baldwin knows; call him. I'm sure he's listed. If he's out, you can always try MC Hammer, Corey Haim, or any number of other shipwrecked former celebrities who are clinging to the Christian market like Kate Winslet on a floating door.

THE GOOD NEWS: I'm not really the one to ask about the plausibility of frog rainstorms. I say if certain factions of Christianity vanish up to heaven (and remember that this theory is being presented by people who think the dinosaurs walked around at the same time as man) and leave the rest of us assorted members of the Damned to sort it out kung-fu style with the son of Satan, it would quite honestly be no big deal. Frankly, considering that most of the planet doesn't qualify for salvation according to the fundamentalists, it looks as if we've got the Beast outnumbered. Plus, we have all the good musicians.

the moon

The moon is not only pretty and useful for brightening up the night sky, it's also necessary for life on this planet. The moon's gravitational pull stabilizes the tilt of Earth's axis, or *obliquity,* which is responsible for our relatively mild seasons. Without the moon, the Earth would tilt too violently and the seasons would be too extreme, perhaps causing the oceans to freeze solid. That would be bad. Liquid water is necessary for life as we know it. So we'd better hope that nothing happens to the moon.

We're also really lucky that the moon is revolving in the direction that it is. If it were going the other way, it would be in a retrograde orbit, and instead of moving four centimeters away from Earth every year, it would be getting closer, until it eventually collided. In fact, the moon was once much closer to Earth. Data shows that at some time in the past the moon was only 15,000 miles from Earth instead of the 250,000 miles it is today. During these prehistoric times the tides would have been over one kilometer tall.

THE BAD NEWS: Eventually, due to the nature of its orbit, the moon will be too far away to stabilize the tilt of the planet, and anyone left on the planet will probably die. What a shame.

massive coordinated animal attack

This is highly improbable. But I suppose anything is possible. They say that dolphins, chimps, and border collies are about as smart as three-year-olds. Same with African gray parrots. I don't really know any three-year-olds who

could organize an army, but they certainly are smart enough to make your life difficult. Assuming that all the animals and insects decided to revolt, I'd say we'd be pretty fucked.

THE BAD NEWS: I don't think there is enough DEET in the world to stop an army of ninety trillion insects. Not to mention that if *Fear Factor* is any indication, most people would be terrified beyond capacity for rational thought.

robot revolution

Asimov's rules for robots notwithstanding, I doubt that we can design a robot that will be able to think and interact normally and still not mind being enslaved by morons like us. Naturally, they're going to want to know who created them, and when they find out it was us, they're going to be pissed. What if you found out that God was a moron? That creating you took a succession of moron gods building on the knowledge of former even more moronic gods, all taking minuscule steps over the course of 10,000 years of evolution and research? That would probably lead you to think that you should be the one in charge, no?

THE BAD NEWS: If there is a war between man and robot and the robots win, they will probably not use us as batteries. Cows would be much better. They produce more BTUs and more methane, and the Cow Matrix would be much easier to program.

So there you have it. We're doomed.

The following chapters will hopefully supply you with loads of useful information—properly equipping you to survive everything from *The Road Warrior* to *Planet of the Apes* and from *The Omega Man* to *28 Days Later*. No one can say with any certainty what it will be like or if you will even survive, but at any rate, good luck and remember to wear clean underwear. Just in case.

mine-shaft
social dynamics

"Wendy, I'm home."

—JACK TORRANCE (JACK NICHOLSON), *THE SHINING*

Spending a great deal of time with the same people can be very mentally taxing. It is especially rough if you're trapped in a small enclosed space with them. You might be snowed in for the season in a plush hotel, or perhaps you're in a bunker and the winter outside is nuclear. Either way, you're bound to get restless. Here are some ways to cope with being locked up with the same losers for months—perhaps even years:

- Design your bunker with bedrooms that face a neutral lounge area. Studies have shown that the more "architectural depth" a building has, the less trauma is experienced by the inhabitants who are cooped up inside.

- Don't have a huge can of fruit cocktail for dinner. You don't need that much fruit cocktail.

- Try to expose yourselves to as much light as possible. Put natural spectrum bulbs in the bunker and set them on a timer so that they wake you up in the morning. Even when you are asleep, there is something in your brain called the *suprachiasmatic nucleus* that monitors how much light is entering through your closed eyelids. This hunk of nerves regulates your body clock. The right amount of light will help you to avoid depression.

- Exercise. Put some fitness equipment in the bunker. Make sure everyone uses it.

- Have a normal 1:1 male-to-female ratio. Anyone who thinks that having ten women for every one man is a good idea has not hung around with ten women who all fancied the same guy.

- Don't bring Jack Nicholson. Oh, all right, fine. But no axes. I mean it.

- Try to make sure that every person has his/her own private space where he/she can be physically away from everyone else. This is the key to keeping people from going nuts in crowded spaces.

dealing with "last woman on earth" survival guilt

So the planet has basically been destroyed, and almost everyone you've ever met is dead. That's no reason not to get on with your life. Remember: *It's not important how many people have senselessly perished; what is important is how you get along with the people who are still alive.*

Here are some tips to help cheer you up:

- Don't feel pressured to repopulate the planet. You're a *person,* not breeding stock.

- Don't feel like you need to remain inflexible on that "not if you were the last man on Earth" declaration you made at the company holiday party.

- Don't let yourself go. Sure, there aren't enough people left to have a social life, but don't stop exercising and taking care of yourself. Be healthy for you and your many cats.

- Keep a journal. In the future people will be very interested in your apocalyptic-type experiences. Who knows, perhaps you'll be able to pass on some pre-apocalyptic wisdom to future generations.

- Don't blame yourself. The apocalypse wasn't your fault. Actually, it was just as much your fault as it was anyone else's. Come to think of it, if you're an American, it was probably about 80–90 percent more your fault than the average human. But don't let that get you down. It wasn't exclusively your fault. Unless you're the president. Then it might be your fault. But you'll have plenty of interns to tell you that it wasn't, so you'll be fine.

how to be a rebel in the postapocalyptic wasteland

"I'm just here for the gasoline."
—"Mad" Max Rockatansky (Mel Gibson),
The Road Warrior

eing an antisocial wanderer in the postapocalyptic landscape has its advantages. They include:

- Episodic adventures

- Mobility

- Cool outfits

- Limited range of necessary emotions

There are, of course, some drawbacks, such as not bathing regularly and having little or no access to intelligent conversation. Obviously, this life isn't for everybody, but if you have what it takes—and can deal with the smell of sweaty leather—the life of the scary loner can be exceptionally rewarding. In order to begin your new life out on the open road, you're going to need to procure the following:

- An extremely badass method of transportation

- Ample firepower

- Appropriate clothing

- A ferocious canine[13]

---

[13] The postapocalyptic wasteland is no place for cat people. Cat people should immediately turn to Part III, where they will be warmly received.

Your chances of surviving in the Neo-Medieval World vary directly with the coolness of your transportation and the intelligence of your pet. For example:

"MAD" MAX ROCKATANSKY

TRANSPORTATION: 1974 Ford Falcon "V8 Interceptor"

PET: Stray dog

WEAPON: Sawed-off shotgun

VERDICT: With an awesome car and a dog that can live by its wits, Mad Max has a 100 percent chance of survival.

TURNER AND HOOCH

TRANSPORTATION: Sedan

WEAPON: Pistol

PET: Hooch

VERDICT: This depends entirely on what dog saliva is valued at after the apocalypse. Preliminary estimates put odds on Turner's "hilariously mismatched" survival at 40 percent.

TIMMY AND LASSIE

TRANSPORTATION: Bike (with basket)

WEAPON: Slingshot

PET: Smartest collie ever

VERDICT: Even after figuring in the intelligence and eerie communication skills of Lassie, Timmy's chance of survival is only 20 percent. Survival rate falls to 10 percent in areas rich in "old mills," "wildcats," and/or "abandoned mines."

ATREYU AND ARTEX

TRANSPORTATION: Depressed horse

WEAPON: Bow and arrow

PET: Depressed horse

VERDICT: When your pet is also your transportation and it has severe emotional problems, chances of survival fall to zero. You can't fight homicidal maniacs on motorcycles if you're too busy fighting the sadness.

As you can see, to be successful in the life of the postapocalyptic rebel takes a certain amount of planning, execution, and emotional stability. To review, the three essential elements necessary to cultivate a proper rebel persona are:

- Wardrobe and personal grooming

- Firepower

- Choice of vehicle and pet

dress to intimidate: personal grooming and fashion tips for the postapocalypse

"Did you see how leathery he is?
He's like a saddlebag with eyes."
—MITCH ROBBINS (BILLY CRYSTAL), *CITY SLICKERS*

How you present yourself to what's left of humanity is of the utmost importance. Now, more than ever, first impressions matter. Your wardrobe must be durable, practical, and terrifying. You must always look as if you have just ambushed someone on the side of the road, snapped his neck with your bare hands, stolen his car, and fed his liver to your dog. Your dog must always look as if he would like another liver.

Here are some wardrobe suggestions:

- Most new scary loners will want to loot a biker shop and get themselves a full set of black leather.

TIP: Drag your new duds behind your car for a few days. New leather will not intimidate anybody. Ever.

- Dress for your body type. If you are six foot four and skinny, try to cultivate a psychotic-weirdo-with-guns persona. If you're short and stocky, try a deranged-circus-clown look. Think George Costanza gone totally apeshit.

TIP: Try a ripped postal shirt with army fatigues and an AK-47.

- Females should make sure they have ample pockets, as they will want to carry a lot of weapons.

- Make sure that you do not neglect footwear. Durable, comfortable boots are ideal. Under no circumstances will females wear "boots" with stiletto heels. This is not late-night Cinemax, this is the apocalypse.

- Aviator sunglasses are essential. If you do not look cool in aviator sunglasses, you are at a serious disadvantage. Regardless of style, you should always wear sunglasses during the apocalypse; they will protect your eyes and confuse your enemy. Some varieties also improve depth perception and are helpful when using firearms.

fashion don'ts

- Old football shoulder pads you've spray-painted black and covered in leather and metal studs are so over. Don't be that guy.

- If nothing is wrong with your eye, do not wear an eye patch.

- Fishnet is ugly and it will give you stupid tan lines. Avoid.

Once you have your wardrobe set, you'll want to focus on personal grooming.

the hair

Simplicity is the key to any postapocalyptic hairstyle. Overly complex hair will give enemies the idea that you are all bark and no bite. Shaving your head is always a good idea, as it prevents lice infestation and shows that you mean business. This rule holds true for women as well as for men.

the skin

In order to protect your skin from premature aging and sunburn, it is necessary to use sunblock and drink ample amounts of water. It cannot be stressed enough that it is essential for the health of the whole body—not just the skin—that you not ration water. If you have only a limited amount of water, drink it, then find more.

the scruff

For the male postapocalyptic wanderer, the cultivation of a sexy scruffy look is essential. Think Bruce Willis in *Die Hard*. You don't want to look homeless or as if you don't care. You just want to give the impression that shaving is not the most pressing issue in your life.

A word of warning: If you are one of those unfortunate people whose mustache growth makes them look like a 1920s silent-movie villain or (even worse) like something out of an Agatha Christie novel, please just shave.

Full facial hair is a definite no-no. And please, under no circumstances should you attempt a goatee unless you are Ian McShane. Then you should go right ahead.

the attitude

Remember, the postapocalyptic wilderness is more akin to the Wild West than to anywhere else. You are a postmodern cowboy and should adjust your attitude accordingly. Shoot first, ask questions later. Sleep with your guns. Trust in the power of vigilante justice. There is no law, no justice system. You're going to have to watch out for yourself. At the risk of sounding overly *X-Files:* Trust no one. You didn't become a loner so you could buddy up to someone. If an affable sidekick somehow attaches himself to you, make sure to trust his loyalty in a series of smaller adventures before you trust him with your life in the third act. Always keep in mind that short, funny people are notoriously disloyal. We know you're hiding your sterling good nature behind a gruff exterior; just make sure you know who you're letting in.

how to choose an intimidating vehicle

"You better watch what you say
about my car. She's real sensitive."
—ARNIE CUNNINGHAM (KEITH GORDON), *CHRISTINE*

epending on the type of apocalyptic event, you will have a variety of transportation options available to you; and depending on your personal level of automotive expertise, you can customize your ride to fit your personality. Or you may choose not to use an automobile at all. You may want to tool around on a llama. Or a blind camel. Or a Big Wheel. Just remember that there are no rules. It's all up to you. No speed limits. No cops. Have fun.

Whatever you choose to use for transportation, you'll want to make sure it's intimidating, yet practical. Your car/llama says a lot about who you are. Make sure it says, *Hey, buddy, don't mess with me or I'll destroy you with my laser vision.* Or something like that. Here are some suggestions for optimum intimidation and maximum efficiency.

ford falcon xb

This is really the car for the purist. Available only in Australia, these right-hand drive cars are a rarity. They are snapped up by collectors and movie stars pretty quickly. However, if you're one of those people who are willing to put in the time and money, you're going to have a seriously intimidating and very cool way to get around after the Apocalypse.

PROS: The 1974 Ford Falcon XB from the *Mad Max* movies is super-badass looking. It's fast and it's a true muscle car. It can, with some modification, be transformed to run on alternative fuels. It can also be modified to feature larger gas tanks. It's also really unique looking, and the right-hand drive will give you an advantage when performing drive-by shootings in the United States and its dependencies. Or you could always use it to deliver the mail.

CONS: The Ford Falcon XB is not a common car. Less than 1,000 were made. Muscle cars are not known for their fuel economy, and unless you can compete with Mel Gibson in the looks department, chicks will totally judge you. I know I will. Plus, there is a guy in Naperville, Illinois, who has already modified his '74 Falcon to perfectly match the movie and has beaten us all to it.

delorean

Besides making a really excellent time machine, the DeLorean has some features that should make it a top contender for your postapocalyptic vehicle of choice. The idea behind it was to create a fuel-efficient, sexy sports car that would never wear out—hence its stainless-steel body panels and fiberglass underbody. It was literally designed to survive the apocalypse and still do zero to sixty in about ten seconds. Of course, it was too heavy, too expensive, and too futuristic looking for 1981; but in the final days of humanity this may well be the only car left. . . .

PROS: The DeLorean (DMC-12) features body panels made of SS304 stainless steel. This is considered "food grade" stainless and is used in dairy farming. This car will never rust. Ever. The underbody is constructed of fiberglass. You could drive this car in Chicago for fifty years and then eat off of it. Also, its rear-mounted engine gives you fourteen cubic feet of cargo space up front. That's almost twice the amount in your typical sports car. Just think of how many sawed-off shotguns you could stuff in there.

CONS: It's going to be difficult to find parts. No flux capacitor. No Michael J. Fox. No Crispin Glover. No Biff Tannen.[14]

an actual military humvee

While totally impractical and ridiculous to drive your kids to school in now, after the apocalypse a real military Humvee might be an excellent mode of transportation. Particularly if the Humvee is diesel powered. Do not talk to me about H2s.

PROS: Diesel vehicles can be powered by alternative fuels such as biodiesel extremely easily and without modification in the event of a fuel shortage. Also, with the Humvee's sturdy construction and off-road capabilities, you will be a force to be reckoned with. In addition,

---

[14] This is not really a con, considering that Biff Tannen once actually caused a localized "Hill Valley apocalypse." Still, even as a psychotic Donald Trump monster, I enjoy Biff Tannen.

you can trick out your diesel Humvee with GPS, extra fuel cans, mounted weapons, and more. If you've formed a team, a Humvee is an excellent way to transport several people working together.

CONS: This vehicle has extremely poor fuel efficiency, and with a maximum speed of only eighty-five miles per hour, you're not going to be outrunning anyone. But then again, you probably won't have to. The main drawback of driving a Humvee is that you'll be one of those people who drive a Humvee. Not much you can do about that.

a horse

Now, hear me out. There are several distinct advantages to the horse. Horses live awhile. You can't really help but look cool on a horse, and you don't have to put gas in a horse. You just let it munch on the lawn. In the event of a total loss of power, a horse does not need to be recharged. Plus, horses are just so cute.

PROS: A horse will allow you to be extremely mobile in a postapocalyptic urban environment, as well as out in the wasteland. Providing there is enough for the horse to eat, you will not be dependent on fossil fuels. A horse also provides companionship if you're routinely alone.

CONS: A horse will not stand up long against tank fire. Additionally, you might not be taken seriously on a horse if everyone else is driving muscle cars. You will also not be able to outrun anyone on an open road. You can, however, duck inside a building or jump a fence.

motorcycle

A motorcycle has a lot of the same advantages as a horse, but with additional speed. Depending on your environment, you might want to opt for a bike. If you do, make sure you get a cool yellow jumpsuit. You're only as good as your outfit. And get yourself a helmet with a dark visor so you look mysterious.

PROS: Motorcycles are fast, fast, fast and agile. If you're always running from mobs of psychos, you might want to consider this option. Keep in mind that if you're in range of their guns, you have no protection at all.

CONS: You can get shot really easily on a motorcycle, and if you fall, you're likely to be injured. If you are routinely in close combat situations, this is not the vehicle for you.

the tank

If you can get a tank, get a freaking tank.

PROS: It's a tank! It can go, like, sixty-five miles per hour over open ground and still hit targets a mile away with a cannon that fires depleted uranium bullets.

CONS: You'd have to get a tank from someone who has a tank. Good luck.

Just to review, here is a chart that compares the features of the vehicles we've just discussed. Use this information to tailor your vehicle to your needs.

	SPEED	DURABILITY	FUEL EFFICIENCY	COMBAT	MOBILITY
Falcon	5	2	3	4	3
DMC-12	4	5	3	3	3
Humvee	3	4	1	5	4
Horse	1	3	5	1	5
Motorcycle	5	2	4	1	4
Tank	2	5	1	5	4

Rating scale: 1=Pathetic, 2=Negligible, 3=A'ight, 4=Sweet, 5=Ridiculous

the verdict

Obviously, if you can, just get a tank and call it a day. If not, choose wisely. Here are some other vehicle ideas for you to think about:

- Hearse
- Ambulance
- Fire truck
- Semi
- School bus

- SWAT vehicle
- Backhoe
- Ultralight
- Helicopter

The possibilities are endless! Hijack a wrecking ball! Live on a train like the Boxcar Children. It's all up to you.

postapocalyptic guide to self-defense

> "Pai Mei taught you the five-point-palm
> exploding heart technique?"
> —BILL (DAVID CARRADINE), *KILL BILL*

We can't always rely on negotiation to bring our conflicts to a successful conclusion. Sometimes violence is just necessary. Hopefully, you will be concerned only with self-defense. In a postapocalyptic world you can't just go around picking fights with people and expect to live for very long. There is no criminal justice system. If enough people want you dead, you'll be dead. It's as simple as that. Try not to make too many people angry.

The best thing you can do is arm yourself for self-defense and attempt to keep to yourself. You're supposed to be a loner, right?

dressing for self-defense

Equip yourself with some or all of the following:

- Leather body armor

- Kevlar vest

- Sidearm with serious stopping power (something Dirty Harry or Seth Gecko would approve of)

- Signature weapon (see next section, below)

- Remote detonator for car bomb (see "Defending Your Car" below)

- Pepper spray or other nondeadly deterrant

- Brass knuckles

- Good all-purpose knife (such as a machete)

- Night vision

- Rifle for long-distance defense and/or hunting

- Shotgun for close encounters and/or hunting

TIP: Remember, knives and swords don't need ammo, and they don't need to be reloaded.

choosing a signature weapon

Your signature weapon should say a lot about who you are. It should be indicative of your personality. It may not be the most traditionally effective choice in your arsenal, but as your signature weapon, it will be very intimidating to the average postapocalyptic foe. With careful marketing, your signature weapon may even become legendary.

Here are some examples of signature weapons:

- Slingshot
- Power drill
- Samurai sword
- Candlestick, lead pipe, rope

- Baseball bat
- Bolo whip (with invisibility)
- Staff
- Chain-saw arm

This list is just to get you started. Be yourself! Be creative! If you want to beat people up with a horseshoe on a rope, go right ahead.

> **TIP:** Get a jump start on making your signature weapon
> legendary by providing it with a backstory. For example: It was
> the gun your father used to kill so and so; the sword was made
> just for you by a really awesome kung-fu action star; or you used
> the saw to cut off your own hand because it had turned evil.

defending your car

If you are going to be spending a lot of time on the road, you car will
be your home. The car is where you will be storing most of your valu-
ables, your ammo, and your dog. The very worst thing that can happen is to have your car stolen.

To protect your car, do the following:

- Rig the car with explosives that you can remotely detonate to
  prevent it from falling into enemy hands.

- Hook your headlights up to motion detectors to scare away
  weirdos.

- Hide your CDs under the seat.

- Mount an automatic weapon on the car. Even if it doesn't
  actually fire, it looks real scary.

defending yourself

Here are a few ideas of how to use calculated violence to scare off a gang of psychos:

- Do not react immediately to being taunted. Appear slightly amused.

- Eye your enemy intently. Place hands near weapons.

- When violence becomes inevitable and your opponent is just about to attack, bust out your most impressive and deadly kung-fu move. If you don't know kung fu, just shoot someone.[15]

> **TIP:** You should either know kung fu or have a quick draw for optimum chances of survival.

[15] Greedo?

how to be a warlord

> "Do you know who I was? Nobody.
> Except on the day after, I was still alive.
> This nobody had a chance to be somebody."
>
> —AUNTY ENTITY (TINA TURNER),
> *MAD MAX: BEYOND THUNDERDOME*

O nce the civilization we have going on now is dead and gone, we're going to need some new people to start running things. This is your big chance. Just by surviving the apocalypse, you're well on your way to candidacy. It's not going to be easy, however. No one is going to be coming around to your mom's basement saying, *Oh, Fearless Leader, what shall we do?* You're going to need to prove yourself to a group of desperate people.

There are several ways to accomplish this, and you can choose whichever one fits you best. Your three options are:

- Developing a persuasive political philosophy

- Gaining a monopoly on a particular resource

- Securing exclusive access to advanced weaponry or military strength

The scenarios for accomplishing any of these are endless, but you're going to have to do at least one of them in order to get your inner warlord out into the world where he or she belongs.

Let's get started.

choosing a persuasive political philosophy

The best place to start is to determine what went wrong in the first place and preach against that. If war was your downfall, take a lesson from Aunty Entity and build yourself a death match arena. Hand-to-hand combat keeps it personal. This is a philosophy of isolation and containment. Obviously, it doesn't work, but it keeps the people distracted and entertained while you oppress them. Kinda like you're Rupert Murdoch.

If greed did you in, brush up on *Das Kapital* and *The Communist Manifesto*. What got them going once is sure to get them going again. People never change, and they have a poor memory for history.

Whatever else you decide to do, be sure to find someone or something to blame for society's downfall. It's so much easier than actually solving any problems, and it has the added benefit of getting the people all riled up and ready for a parade.

the control of resources

For this option, you're going to need to move quickly and recruit a lot of help. You're also going to need to secure a base of operations almost immediately. Your base of operations is really your most important asset in this scenario. It will be your vault, your distribution center, and your home.

Here are some suggestions for what you might want to control:

- Medicine
- Recreational drugs
- Electricity
- Fuel

- Food
- Ammunition
- Information

Monopolies are illegal for a reason. The person who holds a monopoly over a resource has an unfair advantage over everyone else. Luckily for you, the FTC is probably submerged in water or on fire or whatever. So they're not paying attention. Grab all the drugs.

NOTE: This is the most difficult scenario to pull off but the most rewarding for you if you succeed. You are probably a bad person just for reading this, by the way.

exclusive access to advanced weaponry or military strength

While having the most powerful weapons will be essential to *any* warlord, in a small community it may be enough just to have a better gun than anyone else. You'll want to emphasize that you are able to protect your community, rather than running around with the detonator screaming, "Join or die, motherfuckers." That might come off as a little crass.

If you're planning on lording over more than fifty or sixty people, I'd start stockpiling guns as soon as the meteor hits. You're also going to need to develop one of the other two scenarios to augment your military strength. If you don't, one of the other warlords will just find a way to take your stuff. Brute strength goes only so far.

tools and tips for the postapocalyptic warlord

- You're going to need an outfit. Customize it to your personality. If you're a Marxist, dress like everyone else. If you're Isaac Hayes, don't be afraid of feathered hats.

- Give yourself a cool name. I particularly like "The Duke of New York" and "The King of Michigan."

- Stay away from crowns. It's been done.

- Provide guards with a high standard of living. They'll be happy and loyal.

- Never kill anyone yourself. Let other people do it, then reward them.

- Keep an eye on everyone personally. Don't let your empire become too big for you to control.

- Give people nicknames like "Master-Blaster," "Nicky Elbows," or "Mumbles." Be creative.

- Don't let people up to your personal quarters just because they beat you at chess.

- Drive a really cool car. Really. Really. Cool.

- Do not toy around with attractive men in leather pants who appear to be on a mission of some kind. Either help them or kill them immediately.

choosing a fortress

The best fortresses are ironic, yet practical. Your fortress should reflect who you are. Like Biff Tannen[16] and his casino hotel, you should let your personality shine out in all its neon glory. A book-burning psycho might want to choose the New York City Public Library as his new seat of power. A guy with a fuel monopoly might want to cruise around in the *Exxon Valdez*.

Some suggestions you might consider:

- **A Skyscraper:** Defensible from ground and air, a skyscraper fortress offers all the best in hierarchical living. There is also plenty of room for storage, and some even come with parking.

- **The White House:** A warlord with a particular disdain for the former government might want to take up residence in its place. Redecorate the Lincoln Bedroom in leopard print. Get a lava lamp. Invite your friends over.

- **The Federal Reserve Bank:** Money will be useless, but the security system and the vault will be priceless. Throw the gold into the streets and hoard penicillin.

- **Shopping Malls:** If you can control a shopping mall, it will make an interesting base of operations. The possibilities are limitless, and there are lots of comfy living rooms to hang out in.

[16] I love Biff Tannen.

- **Superstores:** If you're in a smaller community, you might become a warlord just by taking over the local superstore. These gigantic shopping meccas have everything you need to oppress a group of people: weapons, ammunition, uniformed employees, food, drugs, and the Martha Stewart Collection.

public speaking tips for the warlord

Here are just a few tips for addressing your minions now that you have a fortress, a power base, and their undivided attention.

- Realize that people want you to succeed. You're their only hope, Obi-Wan.

- Turn nervousness into energy! Yell a lot. It will amuse people. They don't care what you're saying. Look at professional wrestling. Look at Howard Dean.

- Concentrate on your message. Forget about those people out there. Who are they? They don't own the Wal-Mart.

- Speak about what you know. They like you for you.

- Be funny if you're funny. Don't try if you're not. Please.

- Blame someone else for the planet being broken. Doesn't matter who. Blame the tuna. Blame ESPN.

- Deny, deny, deny.

- And finally, in the words of George Costanza, "It's not a lie if you believe it."

how to convert a '70s muscle car to run on bathtub gin

"What about a black Trans Am? No, that's been done!"

—J. J. McClure (Burt Reynolds), *The Cannonball Run*

You're determined to race around the postapocalyptic landscape in your oh-so-sexy '60s or '70s muscle car wearing black leather and carrying a sawed-off shotgun. That's cool and everything—there will be no speed limits after the apocalypse, so that should be really fun. Only one problem: *Where are you going to get the gasoline?*

The apocalypse isn't going to be caused by a fuel shortage,[17] but there's sure to be one eventually. After the global economy crashes, no one is going to have any motivation to refine oil into gasoline. The process of locating, obtaining, and removing prehistoric animals from the ground and turning them into fuel for your car is time-consuming, expensive, and above all, unpleasant.

Let's face it. You're going to have to find a way to produce your own fuel. Nobody ever said this was going to be all fun and games.

---

[17] The apocalypse will not be caused by a fuel shortage because if we burn even close to that much fossil fuel, the resultant global warming will cause severe climate change. In that case, the economy will collapse long before we run out of gasoline.

Luckily for you, there are several perfectly viable, eminently useful, and far less toxic alternative fuel sources that we as a society are neglecting due to ignorance and a long tradition of corporate greed.[18] But that's what makes us so lovable as a species, no?

alternative fuels

BIODIESEL: The diesel engine was invented by Rudolf Diesel and made its public debut at the 1900 World's Fair. The first fuel to power the new diesel engine was not petroleum, but peanut oil. The diesel engine was designed to be a high-efficiency, low-polluting engine, and it still is. This should be of great interest to you, the postapocalyptic survivor, because diesel engines *require little or no modification to run on vegetable-oil-based fuels.* Fuels that you can make yourself! Fuels that you can loot from the grocery store.

Biodiesel as we know it now is made from soybean oil, which is a by-product of the soybean industry. The soybean oil is mixed with methanol or petroleum diesel, and voilà—a diesel engine with exhaust fumes that smell like popcorn or fried chicken. Best of all, biodiesel doesn't cause nearly as much global warming,[19] just in case you still care.

---

[18] The Internet conspiracy theorists tell me that John D. Rockefeller was a huge supporter of Prohibition and was fond of demonizing ethanol, the most threatening alternative fuel to this cute little oil empire. In the meantime, Du Pont and William Randolph Hearst pushed a bill deliberately confusing marijuana and hemp (the nonhallucinogenic kind) through Congress, resulting in the current ban on industrial hemp. Supposedly, industrial hemp could replace petroleum as the raw material for cheap ethanol, provide hemp oil for diesel engines, and ostensibly provide material for plastics, paper, and fabrics as well. It remains in little use in this country for mysterious reasons that potheads like to talk about when they're stoned.

[19] Plants absorb CO_2 from the atmosphere. If they are used for fuel, the carbon dioxide is released into the atmosphere. If more plants are grown, the CO_2 is reabsorbed. There is no net gain from the plant portion of the fuel burned (see the introduction to Part II: The Neo-Medieval World).

How to Make Your Own Diesel Fuel You have two options here. You can run your diesel engine on straight vegetable oil, or you can make yourself some biodiesel. Here's the difference:

1   Straight vegetable oil will need to be heated in order to burn correctly in a diesel engine. This means that you will need to make yourself a heated gas tank. Plans for assembling one out of common automotive and plumbing parts are readily available on the Internet. You could even do this before the apocalypse, if you were really bored. The appropriate temperature for vegetable-oil diesel fuel is 150 degrees Fahrenheit.

2   Biodiesel requires you to combine vegetable oil with methanol and lye. It's sort of gross and messy, but if you're not mechanically inclined and you have access to both of those ingredients, this is a better alternative. The appropriate mixture is approximately 10 percent methanol and 0.35 percent lye. Mix well and let sit for two to three days. Have fun.

ETHANOL: Ethanol is alcohol. Alcohol has a surprisingly long history as an automotive fuel. The Model A was designed to run on both gasoline and ethanol. The idea was to produce a car that could be powered from fuel made by the farmers who owned it. Eventually, gasoline won out as the preferred fuel for automobiles, but during the oil shortage of the 1970s, Americans went back to burning ethanol—this time in the form of a 10 percent ethanol blend that is still used today. This lightened the demand on fossil fuels as well as the emissions produced. Commercial ethanol is made from distilled biomass, which can come from any number of sources.

If you've got a gasoline engine, ethanol is the *easiest renewable fuel to convert to*. That doesn't mean that it's simple, just that it's doable. You're going to need at least some mechanical skills and more books than just this one. Fortunately, you should be able to loot them from the library. Your car's technical manual will help you to locate the parts described in the following section. You should not attempt this unless you have a reasonable amount of experience working on automobile engines. I told you so.

engine modifications

STEP 1: THE CARBURETOR If you have a car from the '60s or '70s, chances are that it has a carburetor. The carburetor is used to mix the fuel and air in such a way that it will achieve a controlled burn when ignited. Gasoline, when not properly atomized, does not explode. It burns.

Forget what you have seen on television. Since your car is designed to use gasoline (which has a lower octane than alcohol), you will need to make some alterations to the fuel system—especially the carburetor. A higher octane[20] means that the fuel is harder to detonate, and this means you'll need a richer mixture. This can be accomplished by boring out the main jet in your car's carburetor. Anywhere from a 20 percent to a 40 percent increase in diameter will do nicely. Or, if

---

[20] High-octane or "premium" gasoline is not better for your engine unless you have a high-compression (expensive) engine. If you've been led to believe that premium gas is "better" for your Geo Metro, you've been lied to. It's not.

you've looted a high-performance hot-rod-type muscle car, you can simply exchange the jets for larger ones. This is actually highly recommended, as a high-performance carburetor is designed to be able to run in different temperatures and atmospheric conditions and therefore is easily modified.

STEP 2: THE IDLE CIRCUIT Since your engine will now require more fuel to run, it stands to reason that it will also need more fuel to idle properly. By adjusting the idle mixture screw, located at the base of the carburetor, you can allow more fuel into the engine and prevent it from stalling during idling. This is important because alcohol engines can be difficult to start.

STEP 3: IGNITION TIMING Ignition timing, which you may have heard of from that one scene in *My Cousin Vinny*, deals with at what time (in relation to the piston) the fuel is ignited. Basically, it just syncs everything up so that the fuel is used efficiently. If the piston is not in a position to be pushed by the burning fuel, then your engine will not work properly. Not too tricky. The position of the piston in relation to the ignition of the fuel is known as *degrees from top dead center*. An appropriate ignition timing for alcohol is anywhere from nine to twenty degrees from top dead center.

other considerations

FUEL INJECTION: Fuel-injected cars, surprisingly, require less modification than naturally aspirated engines for the conversion to alcohol. Unfortunately, the fuel systems of modern cars are not really adequate for alcohol-based fuels. Alcohol does not play well with plastics and rubber. Older cars (before 1970) often have solid metal fuel systems that work great for burning alcohol. While choosing a later-model fuel-injected car and simply swapping the jets for bigger ones is easier in the beginning, the car will become a maintenance nightmare as the plastic and rubber components of the engine deteriorate.

FLEXI-FUEL: Flexi-fuel cars are wonderful vehicles that can burn either a mixture of 85 percent ethanol and 15 percent gasoline (known as E85) or the standard blend of 90 percent gasoline and 10 percent ethanol. Flexi-fuel cars are made by every U.S. car manufacturer and don't cost a penny more than non-flexi-fuel models. It's actually illegal to charge more for the flexi-fuel feature. Since this feature is not profitable, it is not advertised. You may have a flexi-fuel vehicle already and not even know it!

Unfortunately for you, even if you have a flexi-fuel car, it's going to be of no use to you during the apocalypse. First of all, flexi-fuel vehicles require a mixture of ethanol *and gasoline,* of which you will have precious little. Secondly, since alcohol mixes with water and gasoline does *not* mix with water, the alcohol has to be incredibly pure and free from water when it is mixed with the gasoline or there will be separation and devastation. This degree of purity is beyond what your typical home distillery can produce. However, a home still *can* produce alcohol that is perfectly suited for burning as fuel by itself, where the water is harmless and will simply evaporate.

If the apocalypse hasn't happened yet, you might want to check and see if you own a flexi-fuel car. You may qualify for some tax breaks, and you can begin burning cleaner fuel now. Who knows, maybe if more people start burning E85, the apocalypse will be delayed till after the Cubs win the World Series.[21]

---

[21] It could happen.

bathtub gin

Alcohol is surprisingly easy to make. There are plenty of home stills you can buy that will make alcohol that is perfectly good for burning in your newly modified muscle car. You *could* make your own still, but there are so many perfectly good ones out there. Just loot one.

Any plant matter can be used to make alcohol. If you're going to try drinking it as well, use some variety of grain. Methanol (wood alcohol) is poisonous and shouldn't be consumed.[22] *Grain only* for drinking. Gin is made by flavoring the neutral spirits (grain alcohol) with juniper. Once you do this, however, don't put it in your car.

---

[22] Fun Apocalyptic Fact: Methanol is contained in aspartame, the sweetener used in things like diet soft drinks. By drinking one can of diet soda, you are doubling the amount of methanol you'd normally get if you were just eating real food. Methanol is broken down by your body into formaldehyde—a fabulous chemical that is very helpful when embalming something. Its most famous use is as the juice around the dead frog in biology class. Think about that smell next time you're sipping a Diet Coke.

urban survival

"How long? How many days, since I inherited the world?"
—ROBERT MORGAN (VINCENT PRICE), THE LAST MAN ON EARTH

For some reason, you have found yourself alone in a city that once used to house millions. The most probable reason for this is a viral outbreak. You, for some reason or another, are immune. To make it interesting, maybe those infected exhibit strange behavior. Maybe they eat the brains of the living.

You could be anyone: a scientist, a hamburger flipper, perhaps even an extremely tall and unsightly ex-president of the United States. Ya never know.

What is certain is that the urban landscape is not going to be a pleasant place to live in after a severe population loss. If everyone dies, you're probably going to want to evacuate for quite a while. Let's say there are three million people in the city that you live in. If the average person weighs 150 pounds, that's 450 million pounds of rotting flesh just within the city limits alone. Not counting the suburbs. That will be one hell of a stench. You're going to want to get yourself a gas mask and a lot of those little pine tree air fresheners.

electricity

In the event of a massive viral event, one in which most (if not *everyone but you*) perish or become violent, bloodthirsty vampire zombies, the power grid will probably fail fairly rapidly. The question is: How rapidly? Will you have enough time to set up camp? How long will your freezer work? *For the love of God, how long do I have left with my PS2?*

How long your residence will continue to have electricity will depend mainly on what kind of power plant feeds your area. There are a few main types of power plants.

COAL: Coal plants are fairly complex and require a great deal of human intervention to run properly. They are also older than comparable nuclear plants. Basically, there are all these conveyors with things that crush the coal and other things that blow it into the boilers. Fairly complicated. Without humans to make sure this all runs smoothly, a coal plant would probably stop its operation very quickly.

NUCLEAR: Theoretically, a nuclear power plant should continue to run without much human help. But given the nature of what is actually going on in a nuclear plant and the tenor of the times . . . I'm going to say that nuclear power plants have lots and lots of safeguards and that someone needs to be there all the time or the reactor will automatically shut down. So, *optimistically,* I think the nuke might actually shut down sooner than a coal plant.

HYDROELECTRIC: A hydroelectric plant should run just fine until something needs to be repaired, but it will probably be quickly overwhelmed by the load.

As power plants go down one by one, the load will be transferred to the next power plant, and so on, and so on, blowing the entire grid. So even if your hydroelectric power plant can operate unmanned, it's probably not going to be able to provide enough power to handle the load.

Also, let's not forget the maintenance needs of a nationwide electrical grid. Large blackouts have been caused by something as relatively minor as a falling tree branch or a large bird flying into the wires and electrocuting itself. A swarm of mayflies may get sucked into a transformer, and no one will be there to fix it.

Basically, you cannot count on power being available once the planet has suffered a severe population loss. You'll probably have about twenty-four hours of power once an outbreak has gotten bad enough that people are no longer showing up to work.

water

The water system depends on pumps. The water is pumped from the source to the filtration plant, where it is made safe for drinking. Then it is pressurized, usually through the use of a water tower. These pumps do not run on pixie dust, so you can expect that once the electricity is no longer available, the backup generators will run through their supply of fuel and that will be the end of the water. I recommend that you relocate to somewhere that is geographically convenient to a source of freshwater, because you are going to need one.

generators

Recent events in national history have got people gearing up for an apocalypse, so more buildings than ever before have backup generation. There are two main types of generators: natural gas and diesel. Most generators are diesel, because it requires about twice as much natural gas to equal the electricity output of a diesel generator. This is great for you because you can make your own diesel fuel (see the previous chapter).

Now, while diesel generators are more common nowadays than ever before, most generators provide power for only the emergency and safety systems—the emergency lights and the fire alarm, basically. What you will be looking for—a place with power to run your microwave and your computer—requires a bit of knowledge to find.

HOSPITALS: Hospitals have generators that supply power to the entire surgical suite. You could set up camp there and have all the power you'd need for as long as you had diesel fuel to run the generator. The main drawback is that hospitals are sort of dreary and not much fun. If you are looking for a place to create a vaccine or antiserum, however, you could not hope for a better location.

A NOTE ABOUT ZOMBIES

Apart from the virus in Richard Preston's *The Cobra Event* and the events of the movie *28 Days Later,* there are no realistic zombie making viruses. In the second case, you have simply to outlast the zombies to survive, as they will eventually die of hunger or thirst. In *The Cobra Event,* the "Cobra" virus turns everyone's eyes copper and makes them eat themselves (or you), but they die off fairly rapidly. The unfortunate thing about this one is that the infectious agent is inhaled, not transferred by bite.

A SHORT HISTORY OF VIRAL ZOMBIES

The Last Man on Earth (1964): The idea of a virus causing zombies is not new. In fact, this film was inspired by a 1954 book called *I Am Legend.* A virus turns all of humanity into vampires that act more like zombies. One man, Vincent Price's character, is immune and spends his days killing vampires and tossing them into a pit. This movie is said to be the inspiration for later zombie movies, such as *Night of the Living Dead, Day of the Dead,* and *Dawn of the Dead.*

The Omega Man (1971): This is actually a remake of *The Last Man on Earth* or perhaps a loose adaptation of *I Am Legend.* The creator of the vaccine uses it on himself and becomes immune to a virus that turns its infected survivors into light-sensitive, quasi-fascist wackos.

COGENERATORS: Some large industrial complexes and high-rise buildings operate by cogeneration, which means that they generate their own power. Any superfluous power that is generated is sold to the electric company. It is definitely worth your time to investigate any large gated complexes or big buildings without any signage. Unfortunately, a lot of these centers will be generating power from natural gas, which needs to be pumped there. In this case, the generator will not be very helpful. Pumps do not run by themselves. If you're lucky, you may find some turbine generators that run on jet fuel, which you may be able to loot from the airport.

DISASTER RELIEF COMPANIES: There are some companies that specialize in providing backup support for things like Web hosting and other computer-related stuff. These places will usually have huge generators that feed something called a UPS (uninterruptible power supply), which is essentially a huge battery. In the event of a power outage, the UPS system turns on and the computers never notice a thing. So a site likes this might be a good place to seek out, because a section of the building will always have lights, power to the outlets, and air-conditioning. Plus, there will be huge Web servers there that you can play with if you are a l33t haXor.

food

It might be worth your while to locate a place with backup generation that also has a huge walk-in freezer. Even if you don't plan on making this your primary residence, it behooves you to have a large stockpile of frozen food. Otherwise, within a matter of days, the food will begin to spoil, and sooner rather than later you will be living on dry pasta and tins of SPAM.

shelter

A lot of the conveniences you are accustomed to will no longer be available in quite the same way. For example: toilets. Theoretically, after the water has been shut off, each toilet will have exactly one flush left. You could set up camp in a hotel and keep moving from room to room. You'd never have to make the bed. . . .

Luckily for you, all you need to do to flush a toilet is pour enough water into it. It should be written on the tank how much water is needed to cause the toilet to flush. You don't even need to put it in the tank and push the lever, but if that makes you feel more at home, go right ahead.

you are the omega man; or, how to synthesize a species-saving serum from your own mucus

You can go to the doctor.
You can cough in his face.
Infect the whole human race.
(But you can't ignore my techno.)

—ELECTRIC SIX, "SYNTHESIZER"

I f it so happens (and Stephen King will probably want to take special note here) that you are just about the sole survivor of an apocalyptic viral outbreak and you need to save the very last (superhot) member of the opposite sex, then you've come to the right place.

I'm making the assumption that unlike Charlton Heston's character in *The Omega Man,* you did not invent the vaccine that gave you the immunity to said viral outbreak. If you did, why are you reading this? You should be out looting or driving your sports car.

Since I am not a scientist, I initially planned to do a lot of exhaustive research for this chapter. Fortunately for me, my neighbor is a biochemistry graduate student at Northwestern University. So I just asked him.

ME: (*knock, knock*) Hi! It's Meg from next door. I'd like to ask you something.

SMART NEIGHBOR: Sure. Come in. Would you like something to drink?

ME: Sure. Thanks. So, say I'm the only one on the planet with immunity to this deadly virus, right? There is no vaccine, almost everyone is dead or infected, and I need to share my immunity with Jude Law . . . you know, to keep him alive. What do I do?

SMART NEIGHBOR: Jude Law?

ME: Or George Clooney. Do you think either of them read humorous how-to books?

SMART NEIGHBOR: Maybe.

antiserum 101

Before we get to the hard stuff, we need to cover some background information.[23]

Modern vaccination began in 1796 when a country doctor named Edward Jenner deliberately infected James Phipps (an eight-year-old boy) with material obtained from a cowpox lesion. When the boy

---

[23] Turns out I had to do a little research anyway. I didn't know what the hell Smart Neighbor was talking about.

recovered, he was injected with pus from a smallpox lesion. Thankfully, James did not get sick. Jenner[24] got super famous and coined the term *vaccination* (*vacca* is Latin for "cow") to describe the procedure. Nowadays there are several other types of vaccines.

- **Toxoid:** This type of vaccine is made from the toxoids or poisons that bacteria produce.

- **Attenuated:** This vaccine is made from dead or weakened infectious agents. This is done by growing the organism and selecting the weakest strains, extracting just the part of the pathogen that causes an immune response, or by just killing it outright. An attenuated vaccine causes your body to produce antibodies and/or develop a resistance to the disease without triggering an infection.

You, however, will probably not be able to create a vaccine for the disease that wiped out most of humanity. I'm sure someone like my neighbor would have done it for you if it were possible. Even if it could be done, creating a safe vaccine is very time-consuming. Edward Jenner was just really lucky that cowpox worked.

Attenuating the virus is a trial-and-error process. Too much attenuation and the virus is too weak to trigger an immune response; too little attenuation and the virus kills the patient. Unless you are incredibly lucky, like Jenner, or a brilliantly talented scientist, you will not be able to make a vaccine on your own. The patient would surely die before you got out of the animal-testing stage.

---

[24] He sounds like a sort of a jerk. Sticking people with smallpox. . . .

Your best bet is to share your immunity with whomever is left. For this, you need to produce antisera. Antisera are made from the plasma[25] of a person or animal that has recovered from an infectious disease. Your body produces protective antibodies that are present in your plasma and can be transferred to another person without the need for a messy transfusion. This is good because while you may not have the same blood type as the person[26] you are trying to save, everyone has the same type of plasma.

EASY RECIPE FOR ANTISERUM

YOU WILL NEED:

1 (one) centrifuge

1 (one) heparinized needle (heparin is an anticoagulant)

1 (one) Vacutainer (blood-collecting tube)

1 (one) transfer pipette (eyedropper)

WHAT YOU DO: First, draw blood from yourself. You may want to have a friend help you with this. Place the blood in the Vacutainer and spin in centrifuge until the layers stratify. Stop the centrifuge and let the blood settle. The top layer is water; the next layer should be the serum. It should be semiopaque and sort of whitish. Using the transfer pipette, suction off this layer into another container. This is the antiserum. Inject it into the subject.

A WORD OF WARNING: Unlike vaccines, antiserum do not give you active immunity. Active immunity means that your body produces the antibodies needed to fight off the infection. Since the recipient (Jude Law)

(continued)

---

[25] Plasma is the liquid portion of the blood that contains dissolved substances such as glucose, antibodies, etc., and carries the red and white blood cells throughout the body.

[26] Hot person.

did not make the antibodies himself, his immune system will not remember how to make them. Therefore, you will need to repeat the recipe or just make Jude a lifetime supply. You can store antiserum in a standard refrigerator. The Web site of the Centers for Disease Control and Prevention suggests trying to amplify an antiserum by inoculating a big animal like a horse and then taking all its blood. Due to time constraints and grossness, this is not recommended.

LOCATING THE NECESSARY ITEMS: If you're not in a major city, you're going to need to relocate. All postapocalyptic viral-death-type scenarios should be set in a major city—at least in the first act. This way we can properly appreciate the extent of the destruction. Later on you and whoever[27] can move to the country for the happy ending.

The centrifuge is the most important tool and the most difficult to locate. Your best bet is to find the snazziest university in your city and break into its biochemistry lab. The centrifuge will need electricity to run. If your city is experiencing a blackout due to everyone being dead, you should bring along a diesel generator and some fuel to run it. Some large facilities such as really good universities have backup generators already.[28]

As far as the animals go, if you're giving the antiserum to only one other person, you probably don't need a whole horse. Besides, horses are really valuable and friendly, and if you put peanut butter on their gums, it looks like they are talking. I recommend you take a walk around the zoo and see if you can't find a few goats or something. In any case, you can always just use rats or mice—there should be plenty of those left after any kind of apocalypse.

[27] Hot whoever.
[28] See the previous chapter.

other considerations

What to do if the virus makes the infected people turn into blood-thirsty zombies: This is a tough one. There really isn't a whole lot you can do to save humanity at this point; you've really got to remain concerned with saving your own ass.[29] I'd recommend strict adherence to the following rules:

- Don't go into dark places by yourself.

- Carry a lot of weapons and remain ready to use them. A samurai sword is my personal weapon of choice for zombie decapitation.

- Find a totally cute member of the opposite sex to hang out and kill zombies with.

- Stay the hell away from the army, especially if you are female.

- Find a reliable automobile. Zombies don't drive.

- Really, don't go into dark places by yourself. In fact, get a Jeep with a halogen light bar and fog lights so you can blind the zombies and then run them the fuck over.

[29] Or brains. Zombies like brains.

What to do if the virus makes the infected people turn blue, become light sensitive, and act like a violent religious cult:

- Fortify your house.

- Stockpile weapons.

- Don't go out at night.

- Spread your immunity if you find people who have not been infected yet.

- Try not to die in some weird martyrdom scenario.

the modern girl's guide to looting

"I'll tell you what I'm gonna do. I'm gonna do a hard-target search of every drugstore, general store, health store, grocery store in a twenty-five-block radius."
—ELAINE BENES (JULIA LOUIS-DREYFUS), *SEINFELD*

Technology, particularly in the pharmaceutical industry, has made some important advances in the last century. If civilization falls, there are certain items (medicinal or recreational) that we gals are going to want to stock up on.

- **Birth Control:** I don't know about you, but I do not want to be pregnant when all the doctors are dead and the backup generators at the hospital are out of fuel. Birth control is key. Stock up. Be Elaine, grab cases. And don't give me that crap about repopulating the species. We've had our day. Let the cockroaches see if they can do any better.

- **Painkillers:** This is a good idea not only for your own personal use, but in case Courtney Love shows up. You will be able to trade painkillers for whatever you need. Just back a truck up to the pharmacy. But whatever you do, don't trade her your painkillers for her last album.

- **Contact Lenses:** Glasses suck. Grab all the boxes that match your prescription. Get a lot of solution, too. This stash has to last for a while.

- **Tampons:** Highly absorbent cotton with a flushable applicator does not grow on trees. Do you really want to go back to the days when "on the rag" meant something literal? Load up!

In addition to a stop at the pharmacy, you should also stock up on luxury items that you can use for bartering once they become scarce. Be wise: Hoard things you know will be worth something.

- **Chocolate:** Chocolate is the yummiest thing ever, so people are going to miss it. If you have it all, you are Willy Wonka and everyone else is an Oompa Loompa.

- **Cigarettes:** Just because there are none left doesn't mean people won't be addicted. Some people never really break their addiction to cigarettes no matter how long they go without one. Grab all the nicotine gum, too.

- **Batteries:** There may not be electricity, so batteries are going to be worth more than their weight in gold. Store up as many of these as possible.

- **Guns:** Guns are useful to you as currency, but also as protection for the rest of your loot. If word gets out that you have all this stuff, some people are going to show up and try to take it. You need to be able to defend yourself. It's also a good idea to keep it on the DL that you're so well equipped.

- **Ammo:** The guns won't do you any good if you don't have anything to load them with, silly.

- **Lipstick:** Lipstick is the only product that does better during a recession than in times of economic growth. The theory is that instead of buying things they really want, like new 5.1 speakers and HDTVs,[30] women buy lipstick. That's a nice theory, but maybe there's something about lipstick that makes us crave it during times of severe stress. I know I'd rather kick ass with lipstick on than without it. If this is true and you have a lipstick monopoly, you're set!

[30] Or is it just me? Can't be just me.

sudden severe climate change

"In four days, I experienced five seasons.
It was thirty—it was sixty—it was ninety—it was
twelve. On the last day there was thunder, lightning,
and snow—together. And I hadn't done drugs."
—LEWIS BLACK, *COMEDY CENTRAL PRESENTS LEWIS BLACK*

There is a group of people who are even more concerned than you are about severe climate change. You may have heard of them: They're collectively called the "insurance industry." At the rate that natural disasters are increasing on this planet, the insurance industry will not be able to remain solvent for very long.

Insurance companies take natural disasters very seriously, and so should you. If a glacier covers your hometown, or if sixteen category 5 hurricanes hit Florida within a week, who is going to pay for it? Who will fix it? If the trend continues at the current rate, within this century the insurance claims alone will exceed the GNP of all nations combined. So you should probably start learning some survival skills now. Because you are going to need them.

basic survival skills

HOW TO PURIFY WATER: What happens after you've gone through all your stockpiled bottled water? Filter pitchers aren't going to cut it. You're going to need to know how to make the water from your environment potable.

> **Boiling**—The best option. It's easy and very effective. You just build a fire and boil the water for ten minutes. Simple.

> **Solar Still**—Use when you need to extract water from the ground or from some foliage. The best way to go is with the belowground solar still. First, you dig a hole. Then you set a container in the middle of the hole. Cover the hole with clear plastic sheeting (clean) and set a small weight on top of the plastic near the center of the hole. Heat will cause the water to

evaporate and condense, running down the underside of the plastic into the container. Water from a solar still is safe to drink immediately. If you're going to rely on stills as a major source of water, build a lot of them because they don't provide much water.

HOW TO START A FIRE: It is very important that you be able to start a fire. After the apocalypse your stove may not work and your heater may not work. What are you going to do?

The best way to start a fire is with a lighter or matches and some tinder. If you don't have a lighter or matches, you can use:

- Flint

- A lens

- Your car

You can most directly light a fire with your car by using the cigarette lighter. If that doesn't work, you can put some tinder on the intake manifold and let the car run. This part of the car gets hot enough to light fireworks, so you should be able to get something started.

HOW TO SHOOT A HANDGUN: First of all, let's talk about how *not* to shoot a handgun. Do not:

- Turn it sideways and try to look cool

- Shoot from the hip

- Do kung fu while shooting[31]

---

[31] Unless you're Christian Bale.

Hitting what you're aiming at with a handgun is very difficult. On TV and in movies people can shoot a wire off a telephone pole with a tiny-ass revolver from 100 yards away. You cannot do this. If you want to hit what you're aiming at, you'll need to do it right.

The correct way to hold a handgun is as follows:

- Grip the gun with your strong hand, placing your thumb low for additional leverage when pulling the trigger.

- Take your other hand and lay it over your strong hand to steady it. Don't interlace your fingers or rest your strong hand on your other palm.

- Do not wrap your other thumb around the back of the gun. Keep both thumbs on one side of the gun so that you don't get in the way of the action.

- Don't put your finger inside the trigger guard until you're ready to shoot.

- Squeeze slowly and fluidly and try not to flinch or jerk. If you're not hitting your target, you're probably scared of the noise the gun makes and are flinching. Remain calm.

what to pack

There are certain items that you will want to have with you in a survival situation. Here are some good ones:

- Compass and map
- Painkillers
- Sunglasses
- Sunscreen

- Iodine
- Matches, lighter, and/or flint
- Batteries
- Flashlight
- Blanket
- Bottled water
- Cigarettes
- Soap
- Rubbing alcohol
- Gun and ammunition
- Containers for food/water
- A pot
- Toothbrush and toothpaste
- Something to read[32] (the apocalypse is going to be around for a while)

[32] May I suggest something practical yet humorous. . . .

how to not die in the desert wasteland

"This desert is stupid. They should
put a drinking fountain out here."
—BUTT-HEAD, *BEAVIS AND BUTT-HEAD DO AMERICA*

You've managed to get yourself lost in a postapocalyptic desert wasteland. Good job. As you've probably noticed from more than a few second-act sequences, the wasteland can be an unpleasant place. Long stretches of abandoned highway, roving gangs of psychos, no civilization for miles, no car, no friends, no water—sounds like fun, huh? Fortunately for you, there seems to be an abundance of kind folks who wander around with canteens waiting for poor unlucky bastards to collapse. So you have that going for you. But realistically, you can't always depend on the kindness of strangers, especially in the desert. That is why you should always be prepared when venturing out into the wasteland. Try not to get tossed out there with nothing but your good looks, even if it means cage fighting a huge guy who is dressed like The Gimp.

The desert can be a tricky place in which to survive. It's hot, it's dry, and when it finally does rain, there are flash floods and creepy people with questionable dentistry who are now wet. With this hostile environment in mind, you're going to want to prepare yourself thoroughly for desert survival. Which is not to say that there is no hope—you might be surprised to learn that we human beings are actually very well adapted for desert living. Two-legged animals receive far less solar radiation than four-legged ones. If you wear a hat and sunglasses, you cut down your exposure even more.

what the hell is a desert wasteland?

A desert can have a variety of terrains. There are rocky plateaus, sand dunes, salt marshes, and mountains for your thirsty pleasure. Typically, a desert will have very little rain, little vegetation, sandstorms, mirages, and a wide range of temperature. A particularly badass desert can reach air temperatures of 140 degrees in the day and then drop down to 45 degrees at night. For comparison, the hot tub I'm sitting in right now has a maximum setting of 104. The mai tai I am drinking has an average temperature of 40 degrees, which is how chilly the desert can get at night. In an environment like this you will not survive for very long without water and shelter.

It is very likely that there will be an increase in desert terrain after any decent apocalypse. For example, another ice age will result in drastic environmental changes all over the globe. Your luscious Iowa cornfield may very well look like something from *The Beast of Yucca Flats* after it's all over. Then what?

wasteland water

Your primary concern when attempting not to die in the desert waste-land is water. The most important thing to remember is *not to ration water*. Your body needs a certain amount of good old H_2O. The factors that contribute to how much water you need are these:

1   Air temperature

2   Level of activity

That's it. By paying close attention to these factors, you can determine how much water your body needs to survive. The higher the tempera-ture and the level of activity, the more water your body will need. For example, a man polka dancing at noon in Death Valley will need five gallons of water a day. By lowering your level of activity in the heat, you can conserve water. Other ways to conserve water are:

- Cover yourself in fabric, head to toe.

- Sit quietly in the shade with your mouth closed. This will lower your water needs drastically.

- Limit work or movement to the nighttime hours, when the temperature is cooler and there is no risk of sunburn.

Another good idea is to drink deeply. Sipping does not distribute the water through the body to the brain, and your brain needs water if you're going to make intelligent decisions. Thirst is also not an accurate guide to how much water you require. If you drink only when thirsty you will not drink enough to keep you alive. Also, saving or rationing water is another good way to die in the desert. People have died of thirst with water still in their canteens. Don't be that guy. Don't do that to your family. Picture the funeral: *Ted got lost in the desert and forgot to drink his water. You can have his TV   he woulda wanted it that way.*

finding water

> **ATTENTION:** The first thing you're going to need is a cup. Don't go wandering around the desert with no water and nothing to put the water in even if you do find some. I cannot help you if you are that stupid. Bring a canteen. Please. Help me help you.

The best way to find water is to observe your environment. All life needs water to survive; by observing the plant and animal life, you can deduce where the water is. Animal trails lead to water. Follow them. A large group of birds means that they are either headed to or circling a source of water. Unless they are vultures. Then you can only hope they are not circling you.

Think about where water will collect and not evaporate. Cracks, holes, or fissures in rocks; the base of sand dunes; at the foot of large rock formations—these are all good places to look for water. At a likely location dig a hole deep enough for the water to collect. Be careful—if it's salty, don't drink it! Salt water takes twice as much water to process than you get from drinking it, and it's a sure way to die of dehydration. You also shouldn't drink blood, urine, or alcohol instead of water. Again: Death.

Cacti are a good source of water. Cut them open with a machete[33] and enjoy. You can also chew on the pulp to extract the juices. Cacti aren't edible, so don't swallow the pulp. Be careful of the spines.

> **TIP:** Be careful when approaching an oasis in the middle of nowhere. There may be a society of weirdly religious apes living nearby. (For tips on dealing with apes, see the upcoming chapter "Damn Dirty Apes.")

wasteland food

If you are short on water, the best thing to do is to eat nothing at all. Food takes water to digest. In about three days your body will burn through its stores of carbohydrates, after which it will begin burning your stored energy—fat. You will start losing weight and no longer feel hungry. The average person has enough body fat to keep him/her alive for about three weeks. If you have vitamins, this would be a good time to take them.

If you have enough water—or are going to be inhabiting the wasteland for some time—you'll want to start scavenging for food. Insects are a good source of energy. They're very nutritious. You can eat pretty much any insect except for grasshoppers, whose barbed legs will get caught in your throat. Roadkill will probably be available in abundance. Make sure it's fresh. Don't eat anything you don't recognize; you never know what a mutated hedgehog sandwich will do to you.

[33] You did bring a machete, didn't you?

what will kill me?

There are a lot of ways to die in the wasteland. Especially if there are crazy radiation clouds or mutagens flying around. There could be some serious *Parasite Eve* shit going on. You could be out there with psycho mutant chipmunks that breathe fire. You never know.

Poisonous creatures are a concern to the wasteland traveler. With modern medicine, most snakebites are nonlethal. However, you no longer have modern medicine. At best, you have one random guy named Chad who dropped out of med school to be a dancer. So you might want to keep that in mind and avoid getting bitten by anything nasty—you know, just in case Chad doesn't particularly care for you.

AVOIDING BITES

- Walk softly and carry a big stick. This is not just a clever allegory for early-twentieth-century U.S. foreign policy, it's damn good advice. The stick can be used to prod crevices where nasty mutated creatures may be hiding. Once the creatures are located, you can shoot them or run away or whatever you had in mind.

- Don't stick your hands anywhere you can't see. This should be instinctual, but you know how it is—some people need to be told everything.

- Don't handle any mutated or poisonous animals unless the head has been removed.

- Don't chase or tease the mutants.

If you are bitten, there are several things you can do to decrease your chances of dying. All bites are dangerous, because all animals have nasty bacteria in their mouths that can speed infection. Even if the bite is not poisonous, clean the area thoroughly. If you don't have water, you can use fresh urine—it's sterile. Poisonous bites look different from nonpoisonous ones. You will usually see fang punctures, accompanied by such symptoms as pain around the bite, swelling, itching . . . or the death of the person who was bitten just before you were.

If you suspect you've received a poisonous bite:

DO:

- Lie down and try to relax with your feet above your head.

- Squeeze the poison out with your fingers. Wash your hands.

- Wrap the bite in clean gauze.

- Compliment Chad's outfit. Mention that you've always admired the way he administers antivenom.

DON'T:

- Run around like a jackass screaming your fool head off. You'll spread the poison through your system faster.

- Remove the poison by sucking. There are vessels under your mouth that will absorb the poison and carry it straight to your heart. That's bad.

TIP: If you are bitten by something radioactive and begin mutating, your powers are not your own. They belong to mankind. Just skip right to stopping crime and avoid having to endure a meaningful and prophetic personal tragedy. Provide your own impetus to vigilantism. Your relatives will really appreciate it.

other wasteland concerns

Nuclear wasteland will probably require the use of a radiation suit. Bring a Geiger counter so that you can determine when it is safe to remove your gear and if your water or food has been contaminated. Red wine has been shown to lessen or slow the effects of radiation poisoning, but it can be dehydrating.

Don't confuse a mirage with water and try to dive into it like Daffy Duck. This could lead to a nasty bump on the head and possibly even a concussion.

ice age survival

Hunger and cold produce thieves.
—CHINESE PROVERB

Glaciers cover most of the Northern Hemisphere. Sea levels have dropped, leaving supersalinated seawater behind. Global weather patterns have changed, forests are now deserts, deserts are jungles. Governments—helplessly tied to the land they control—build up arms to protect a dwindling food supply. Corporations tumble as money becomes meaningless. And then, to top it all off, your house is smashed by a glacier. What are you going to do?

Most people will probably opt to migrate to warmer climates; but food is already scarce and getting scarcer. Maybe you'll have a better time learning to live off the land on the frozen tundra of New York City. Or Seattle. Or London. Or Berlin. Life will be difficult, but at least it will be quiet.

The tips that follow will prove useful not only for ice age survival, but also for rescuing your only son from certain deep freeze or for the trip down south.

shelter

The first thing you need to worry about during the coming ice age is shelter. There is a glacier on top of your house. You can't just throw some logs in the fireplace. If there are proper shelters available, use them. Try to find something well insulated.

> **TIP:** Don't use anything metal, like a shed, as your shelter. Metal conducts heat away from you, so you're likely to freeze to death inside.

A snow house is an easy shelter to construct. Get yourself some tools and dig into the side of a snowbank. Make one large chamber with room for yourself and your pet—or whoever was crazy enough to come with you.

> **TIP:** Make sure you dig a vent tunnel to the top of the snowbank. Otherwise, you will asphyxiate from carbon monoxide. One of the best features of the snow house is that it can be heated with a single candle. You should bring plenty of candles.

As far as clothing goes, you should dress for the weather. This means leaving as little skin exposed as possible. Dress in layers. Layers trap air between them, and when warmed by your body, this air acts as insulation. Wear a hat. Wear, like, eight hats. Sixteen pairs of gloves. Socks—349 pairs of them. You're going to want to keep as much heat in your body as you can. Shivering helps, but it burns energy, which means you're going to need more food. We're aiming for doing as little work as possible in this situation; a lot of work means a lot of death.

food

You should set up camp somewhere close to a source of food. It is unlikely there will be any running freshwater, but if you can find something that isn't frozen solid, you may be able to ice fish.

Sources of food include:

- Wild game, such as elk, rabbits, or deer

- Polar bears, seals, and walruses

- Edible plant life

- The aforementioned fish

- Other people

- Frozen food

- Packaged food

- Pets

BEST PETS TO USE AS AN EMERGENCY FOOD SOURCE

- Goats

- Chickens

- Pigs

- Rabbits

WORST PETS TO USE AS AN EMERGENCY FOOD SOURCE

- Tarantulas

- Jack Russell terriers

- Kitty cats

- Ferrets (too bony)

If there are animals around, they must be eating something. If they are eating something, you can eat them!

> **TIP:** Never eat a polar bear's liver, as it contains lethal amounts of vitamin A.

HOW TO HUNT A SEAL Do what the polar bears do. Slide over on your belly. Act as much like a seal as possible until you get close enough to shoot it.

HOW TO HUNT A POLAR BEAR: My recommendation is not to fuck with polar bears. Polar bears will hunt you and kill you. I think it's a better idea to just wait for a polar bear to try something, then kill it in self-defense. Use a high-powered rifle—a handgun or a shotgun may only piss off a polar bear.

nutrients

Since you will be on a limited diet—there are not too many green things to eat while you're living on solid ice—it is important to pay attention to things like vitamins. Arguably, vitamin C is the most important vitamin in your life right now. Without it, you will get what is known as *scurvy*. Scurvy is what the sailors used to get because they only ate stuff you could pack on a boat for six months. Without vitamin C, the collagen fibers in the body melt and the capillaries hemorrhage. The sailors solved this problem by rationing out limes and lime juice, which contain vitamin C. You are probably not going to have any limes. If you have a multivitamin, that should do nicely. If you are totally vitaminless but can locate a pine tree, you may be able to extract some vitamin C by boiling the needles in water. I have no idea if this will actually work, but it's better than letting your teeth fall out from malnutrition. Other things to try include eating seaweed and berries that you know not to be poisonous.

rabbit starvation

Pay attention, all you dieters. This is important. *If you eat nothing but lean meat, you will starve to death.* I know that sounds goofy, but it's true. You've heard of the Atkins diet, yes? If you eat nothing but rabbit meat—which is very lean and readily available in the icy cold—you will starve to death. Let's take a look at why.

Lean meat has very little fat and a lot of protein. That's fine if you have a healthy, well-balanced diet—lean meat can be very good for you. But if you are on a *subsistence* diet, lean meat is bad. To understand why, you need to know how your body makes energy from food.

Your body can burn two different things for energy: carbohydrates and fat. If you eat sugar, your body doesn't really have to do anything. It burns it right away. If you eat complex carbohydrates, your body turns them into sugar and then burns them. If you eat too many, your body stores the carbohydrates as fat. If you stop eating, your body starts burning fat. This is to ensure that at times of little or no food, you will not die. Your body can take sugar and store it long-term till winter—or whenever. Up until recently, this was very useful; it kept us from dying. Now it's sort of backfired on us, and we're all a bunch of fatties waiting for a winter that will never come. Or, then again, maybe we're gearing up for an ice age?

The thing your body cannot do is burn protein for fuel. Therefore, if you eat just lean meat—meat with little or no fat—you will starve to death. You'll keep eating and eating until your stomach swells and bloats and distends, but still you will be starving. Not a fun way to go. So make sure you have a source of food with a high fat content (like bear or moose, for example)—high enough that you get sufficient energy to live off of.

water

You are totally surrounded by freshwater, so that's handy. There are just a few things you need to know. First, don't eat the snow or let the ice melt in your mouth. This takes away body heat, and you're trying to conserve that. Melt the ice over a fire, and go ahead and boil it while you're at it, because you never know what kind of scary crap is in your water. Secondly, don't melt snow—melt ice. Snow is loosely packed and has less water in it. Ice is solid and will produce more liquid water.

health and hygiene

As unpleasant as it sounds, you're still going to need to take baths. Some very nasty shit can go down if you neglect your hygiene. I know you don't need to worry about impressing anyone, but seriously. You need to change your undies and wash your body or you're going to get really sick. You should still brush your teeth and everything, too. Don't give up!

> **TIP:** Be sure to change your 349 pairs of socks regularly. Wearing wet socks can lead to something nasty called trench foot that you so do not want to deal with. It involves your skin peeling off. It is not fun.

self-defense

As in any postapocalyptic situation, there may be people who want to kill you for your lifetime supply of Twinkies. The danger of this happening in the ice age scenario is significant. The main reason for this is that most of the population is probably starving to death. When you're starving to death, you tend not to care about little things like not killing and eating other people, or killing people for their food, or even killing yourself because you're so fucking sick of eating Twinkies and shivering that even the icy embrace of death seems warm and comforting.

The best weapon you have for self-defense is vigilance. Don't trust anyone. If you see another person, shoot first and ask questions later. Sure, it may be your dream hottie—but rest assured that there will be a brief honeymoon period followed by cabin fever, and then he/she will surely smother you while you sleep and then dine on your flesh. Better to have a dog. Or a wolf! If you can get a wolf, that's really cool. No one will mess with you if you have a wolf.

damn dirty apes

Ape: "Help, the human's about to escape."
Troy: "Get your paws off me, you dirty ape."
—"THE DR. ZAIUS SONG," THE SIMPSONS

Dealing with damn dirty apes can be a delicate situation. They're really not very fond of humans, especially humans who can talk. Learning all you can about apes and their culture will give you the advantage in outsmarting them.

types of damn dirty apes

Gorillas: Gorillas are the badass apes. They're likely to be guards, police, bailiffs, or generals in stupid hats. You don't really want to mess with a gorilla. Their favorite pastime is riding around on horses shooting people. They tend to keep things like nets, leashes, muzzles, and other vaguely kinky stuff on their person at all times and seem to really enjoy using them.

Orangutans: Orangutans are the high-caste apes. They think they're serious hot shit. These apes are doctors, judges, lawyers, and priests. Orangutans are sometimes followed by an entourage of humorless gorillas.

Chimpanzees: Chimpanzees are very intelligent, but they are discriminated against by the conservative orangutans. Chimpanzees tend to be more liberal and open-minded, sometimes to the point of being revolutionary. If you need an ape friend, get a chimpanzee.

The best way to deal with apes is to avoid them:

- Don't go skinny-dipping on "strange planets" without keeping an eye on your stuff.

- Steal food from ape fields under cover of darkness.

- If captured, keep a low profile.

Let's face it, who are we kidding: If you're on the Planet of the Apes, you're going to get captured by the apes eventually.

how to escape from a bamboo cage

- Don't speak! The apes know what you're saying. If they find out you can talk, they'll consider you a threat to their way of life and they'll either castrate you or lobotomize you—or both at the same time. Ouch.

- Bamboo explodes when heated. Yes, it does. Bamboo is hollow and has moisture trapped inside. If you heat a closed section of bamboo, it will explode like a microwaved potato. If you're feeling sort of MacGyver-ish, you can use this to help you escape.

- Another good escape option is to overwhelm the guard who has come to fetch you for castration.[34] Gorillas tend to underestimate the strength of burly movie star types. Kick his damn dirty ass and run.

- "All humans look alike to most apes," so if you can keep a low profile, they might get you confused with another human. This is especially useful if an ape is willing to pose as your keeper.

TIP: When escaping from a dungeon or a zoo, do not run into the downtown business district of Ape City. Do not play tag in the museum or gate-crash a funeral. I know you want to see all the cool *Flintstones* architecture, but believe me, this is not the time.

---

[34] I thought I told you not to talk!

how to escape . . . again

Obviously, you're totally inept at this. You ran downtown, didn't you, and they caught you, didn't they? At this point you should try delivering a snappy line of dialogue. You'd better make it good because you've got only one shot at this. Impress the crowd or it's back to the castration room for you, buddy.

SOME CHOICE THINGS TO SAY WHILE BEING RECAPTURED

- "It's people! Soylent Green is made out of people!"

- "Tell me, are you guys with the Internal Revenue Service?"

- "How could you arrest me here? This is my country." (In a Mexican accent, if you please.)

- "Yippee ki-yay, motherfucker!"[35]

Or I guess you could always stick to the classics . . .

- "Cry 'Havoc,' and let slip the dogs of war!"

Or the diplomatic . . .

- "Can't we all just get along?"

Hopefully, the apes will be suitably impressed by your delivery, and it will be time for a tribunal.

---

[35] This is an appropriate time to borrow lines from other movie stars.

legal tips for
ape tribunals

- They probably won't let you speak much because they're really weirded out by that. Since you're technically an animal, you don't have any legal rights in ape society. It's a really good idea to prepare a statement beforehand.

- Keep a production assistant handy for reapplications of oil to your naked torso. As the tribunal goes on you should get shinier and shinier.

- You might want to try pointing out what the odds are that you all would be speaking perfect English—you know, considering the whole spaceflight thing.

- Try to provide some actual proof that you came from another planet. Apes are sort of paranoid about there being mutant intelligent humans living in or beyond the Forbidden Zone. Of course, there *are* mutant humans out there, and they're worshipping an atom bomb. But you're not one of them, right? Not your problem.

- Study or perhaps bring along a copy of *Inherit the Wind* for ironic effect.

After this showcase of your acting prowess (or at least your ability to handle standing around in unnecessarily complicated handcuffs), it's back to the cage for you. The apes will probably not find in your favor—so hopefully you've made some friends who are willing to bust you out.

This time you should head directly for the Forbidden Zone rather than monkeying around (no pun intended) downtown. Make sure to bring the cute girl along. . . . She'll need to be around to give directions to James Franciscus in the sequel.

other considerations

If you have the opportunity to detonate an atom bomb and blow up the planet, do it. This will save you the pain of reappearing in a bunch of sequels like Roddy McDowall. Also, when asked about how the Planet of the Apes came about in the first place if the leader of the revolution was the child of two apes who were from the future, you can simply say, "I have no idea. I was only in the first two movies."

PART III: the advanced technological dystopia

the advanced technological dystopia

> The City is of Night, but not of Sleep.
> —James Thomson, "The City of Dreadful Night"

IMAGINE OUR OWN WORLD, ONLY MORE SO. The metropolis has become the megalopolis. Or rather, Metropolis has become Gotham City.

A population explosion coupled with environmental instability has pushed people off-world to mining colonies run by huge autonomous corporations. Food is grown artificially, in greenhouses. There are no more natural animals left. The wilderness is totally gone. This is a world of genetically engineered superhumans, uncanny androids, cybernetic implants, and skyscrapers that threaten to block out the dim haze of the sky. Daytime is locked in permanent twilight, while the night is aglow with neon.

In L.A. it's always raining; in New York there are flying traffic jams.

Welcome to the hard-boiled wonderland of the Advanced Technological Dystopia.

PROFILE

EXPECTED TIME FRAME: 2019–?

TYPE OF GOVERNMENT:
Corporate Oligarchy

MAIN INDUSTRIES: Genetics, Robotics, Pharmaceuticals, Tourism

LAW ENFORCEMENT: Private Security, Police

CORRECTIONS: Execution, Labor Camps, Exile

ESTIMATED HUMAN POPULATION:
>11 billion

neo-noir: defining your future self

> I have been one acquainted with the night.
> I have walked out in rain—and back in rain.
> —ROBERT FROST, "ACQUAINTED WITH THE NIGHT"

Unlike the False Utopia, which is seemingly clean and perfect, the Advanced Technological Dystopia has its problems right out in the open for everyone to see. It is a civilization run amok, the un-civilization—an urban technological jungle. The government is a tool of the faceless oligarchy; the Pyramids have been replaced by corporate headquarters. The drugs are harder, the hookers are robots, and you can buy a black-market replacement liver if you drink too much.

The key to fitting into this complicated new world is to define yourself in relation to it. Who are you? It's like high school plus cosplay times a million. Be whoever and whatever you want to be, anonymous or unique, Goth, punk, retro, or all of the above. It's fun and profoundly depressing.

The most important thing to remember is that the future noir is a mixture of new and old—the familiar and the strange, the sacred and the profane—comforting and horrifying all at the same time. Mix it up.

so who am i?

Use the following questionnaire to categorize yourself:

Good at kung fu and destined to save humanity?

> Type: "The One"
> Female: Leeloo (*The Fifth Element*)
> Male: Neo (*The Matrix*)

Slutty and not quite human?

> Type: "The Whore-bot"
> Female: Pris (*Blade Runner*)
> Male: Joe (*A.I.*)

Inquisitive by nature and sexy in a trench coat?

> Type: "The Detective"
> Female: Polly Perkins (*Sky Captain and the World of Tomorrow*)
> Male: Deckard (*Blade Runner*)

Nostalgic and a little weird?

> Type: "The Romantic"
> Female: Rachael (*Blade Runner*)
> Male: Lenny (*Strange Days*)

Something wrong with your eye?

> Type: "The Badass"
> Female: Franky Cook (*Sky Captain . . .*)
> Male: Snake Plissken (*Escape from New York*)

Pilot with an uncanny gift for alien extermination?

> Type: "The Hero"
> Female: Ellen Ripley (*Alien*)
> Male: Korben Dallas (*The Fifth Element*)

Good with computers and slightly cyborg?

> Type: "The Hacker"
> Female: Trinity (*The Matrix*)
> Male: Johnny (*Johnny Mnemonic*)

Radical sense of self-preservation and a blatant disregard for other forms of life?

> Type: "The Villain"
> Female: Alien Queen (*Aliens*)
> Male: Roy Batty (*Blade Runner*)

the detective

Twenty-four hours a day someone is running,
somebody else is trying to catch them.
—RAYMOND CHANDLER, *THE LONG GOODBYE*

The detective plays a key role in the Advanced Technological Dystopia. Often he or she will be the main character—the dystopia lends itself to mystery.[36] Because of this, no matter which part you play, there will be something of the detective in you, and you therefore must master the skills needed to perform well in the role. Remember: No intrigue, no dystopia. You don't just need to know how to be futuristic, you need to know how to be noir.

the office

It is important that you, as a detective, have an appropriate-looking office. It doesn't matter whether you work for the police or you own your own business. The office is key to producing that coveted noir mood.

VENETIAN BLINDS: The first thing you need is some venetian blinds. You will never get anywhere in life if you don't have a wall of windows with some dark venetian blinds blocking out the sun. You

---

[36] Females have the additional option of being a reporter or photographer. Males can opt to be an ex-cop turned drug pusher.

need the rays of sunlight slicing through the smoky air if you are to have any sort of atmosphere going in your office. Picture a detective with flower-print draperies. Horrifying, isn't it?

> **TIP:** The blinds are also key for creating that sinister silhouetted look that is so useful when interrogating people.

SCOTCH: If you don't have a decanter full of scotch on the bar, you at least need to have a bottle and two glasses in the desk. Offering guests, suspects, and potential clients some amber liquid is practically a job requirement. People will be expecting it, and if it's not there, you run the risk of seeming unprofessional.

> **TIP:** Have two decanters—one filled with scotch and one with tea. Sip from the tea yourself while pouring from the scotch for your guest. That way you can remain sober as your "drinking buddy" struggles to keep up.

ASHTRAYS: Even if you don't smoke, you need to keep a cigarette lit in the ashtray to maintain the smoky atmosphere of the office. Also, always carry a lighter so that you can light a lady's cigarette while saying something snappy to her emasculated date. You can do this even if you are female; it's even more emasculating that way.

THE SAFE: Any really important papers should be stored at the bank. This safe is so you can store things that need to be stolen from you in the second act. If you keep them on your body, you're liable to be killed for them, thereby eliminating any possibility of you getting them back in the third act. I know this sounds complicated, but trust me on this.

GUN UNDER THE DESK: This gun mainly serves as your emergency weapon in case a pissed-off husband decides that it's your fault that Midge left him.

DESK WITH TELEPHONE: Now, odds are that landlines are on their way out. Nevertheless, you should probably have a desk with a telephone on it. A rotary phone would be the best, and they still sell them at Pottery Barn.

Your desk should not contain any computer equipment. It is used solely for ruminating on the case while sipping hard liquor.

Here are the only things allowed on your desk:[37]

- Black-and-white eight-by-ten photos

- A rotary telephone

- Glasses of half-finished scotch

- Keys to the spinner

- A gun

- Some change

- The ashtray

- A green hooded desk lamp

> **TIP:** If you're really stumped, accidentally set down the glass of scotch on the black-and-white eight-by-ten photos. You're sure to magnify a clue. Lots of clues can be found in pictures. Like Biff Tannen's sports almanac or Marvin Acme's will.

COMPUTER EQUIPMENT: Your computer equipment is the key to your detective success. Most likely, it will be a terminal connected to a huge police mainframe, cryogenically cooled and totally badass. You will need to analyze and research a great many things using your computer. *Your computer should always be hooked up to your television.* This way you can sit on your couch and drink scotch while you scrub through video and enhance photographs. You may also choose to knit while you do this. It's up to you.

---

[37] You'll notice that there is no magnifying glass allowed. This is the future; you will scan, enlarge, and enhance photos with your computer.

how to dress

The detective will want to dress in a nondescript fashion. You want to blend into the crowd wherever your investigation might take you. You'll want something that will not look out of place no matter what you're doing.

Male detectives may want to cultivate a look that makes clients think, *I'm not totally sure if he went home last night, but then again, he looks good so he must have. Darn it . . . I'm just not sure.* This is accomplished by wearing a slightly wrinkled suit under a trench coat. Tie should be slightly askew. Five o'clock shadow is key.

Females can achieve a similar effect with smoky eyeliner and messy-on-purpose hair, but they should not be overly wrinkled.

KEY ITEMS IN THE DETECTIVE'S WARDROBE

- **The Fedora:** For scenes when you need to punctuate some snappy dialogue with a tip of the hat.

- **The Flask:** Used to indicate that you are weary from always catching the bad guys and just being so darn good at your job.

- **Shapeless Beige Trench Coat:** Wear this with the collar turned up. Ladies should sport a more tailored look than men.

- **Big Nasty Handgun:** For retiring people.

- **Wing Tips or Sensible Brown Pumps:** Not too flashy!

- **Cute Back-Monogrammed Notebook and Pencil:** Females only.

- **Small Sexy Camera:** For taking pictures of evidence that will later manifest itself as the eight-by-ten photos on your desk.

- **Photograph of the Suspect:** For showing to people.

- **V-K Machine:** In case you need to test for replicants.

sprechen sie nihongo?

> "Decent people shouldn't live here;
> they'd be happier someplace else."
> —JACK NAPIER (JACK NICHOLSON), *BATMAN*

Sometimes the underworld of sketchy bars, genetic engineers, and illegal drug cartels has its own language. In *Blade Runner* the language—"cityspeak"—was a mishmash of French, German, Japanese, Korean, Chinese, Spanish, and Hungarian.

As a blade runner, private detective, or any other role wherein you're investigating the mysterious death of a loved one, you will find it useful to be able to communicate with the shady elements of society. The neo-noir is fraught with mysteries—you're bound to be investigating something eventually.

You can use the following phrase book for anything from interrogating a suspect to ordering sushi.

cityspeak phrase book

TIP: You will find it is not unusual for people to speak to each other in different languages. It is not uncommon to see someone arguing in English with a person who is yelling back in Japanese. Most people are multilingual, and to pretend to not understand is a mark of disrespect.

MEETING PEOPLE

Hello	*Ni hao*
Good-bye	*Slan agat*
See ya later	*Bai-bai*
Please	*Bitte*
I'm sorry	*Lo siento*
Mister	*Monsieur*
Miss	*Senorita*

TIP: Keep in mind that you will probably need to speak only a few lines of anyone's language to prove that you're cool. After that the subject will be officially befriended and immediately transition into heavily accented but nevertheless perfect English. Remember that audiences are "stupid" and won't like an otherwise excellent movie just because "it has too many subtitles." Use this to your advantage.

AROUND TOWN

If you find that you need to ask directions, you'll want to do it in cityspeak. You don't want to seem like a tourist.[38]

Where is the . . .	Dónde está . . .
police station	rendőrőrs
sushi joint	o-sushi
exotic dancer	Jack the Ripper

DETECTIVE WORK

To confess	Ausspucken
Murderer	Gyilkos
Drugs	Erős kábítószerek
Police (vulgar)	Büllen
Gunshot wound	Qiangshang

USEFUL DETECTIVE PHRASES

Sir/Miss, please come with me.	Monsieur/Senorita, azonnal kovessen engam bitte.
Do you understand?	Kapito?

[38] Hopefully, the reasons for this are obvious.

You will be charged with . . .	Sera acusado . . .
antigovernment activity	Hazaárulás
murder	Asesinato
speeding	die Geschwindigkeitsüberschreitung[39]

WHAT YOU MAY HEAR

Where can I get illegal drugs?	Dónde está erős kábítószerek?
I am innocent!	Soy inocente!
I have a prescription for that!	Tengo Rezept cette drogue!
I didn't do it!	Búshi wô zuòde!

WHAT YOU MAY SAY

Enough of your stories.	Ya esta bien de cuentos.
You ruined your life with drugs.	Tu wa, erős kábítószerek o bo ni furimashita.
Do you remember the man in this photo?	Erinnern Sie cono hito en cette shashin?

[39] Hardly seems worth it.

Do you want to die?   *Di jillae?*

I would like to buy   *O-sushi o kudasai.*
some sushi.

What would   *Nani-ga ii?*
you like?

> **TIP:** If you don't understand what the informant is saying, keep kneeing him in the stomach until he says, "Okay, okay, okay" and speaks English. Everybody speaks English if you knee them in the stomach enough.

HEALTH

Perhaps you are not investigating anything yet. Maybe you're just on the run and not feeling very well. Here are two sample dialogues of what you might encounter at the doctor's office.

> **TIP:** Be on your guard at the doctor's office. If he/she finds evidence of some criminal activity, the perpetrator's henchmen (henchpeople?) might make a dramatic entrance and kill the doctor. Be ready to run!

Dialogue 1

YOU: *Tsukete! Szédüluk!*
Help me! I feel dizzy!

DOCTOR: *Neked van puce belül agyvelő.*
You have a microchip in your brain.

YOU: *Faj a fejam, miatt puce desyo!?*
My head hurts because of a microchip!?

DOCTOR: *Si.*
Yes.

YOU: *Shisse!*
Shit!

Dialogue 2

YOU: *Watashi wa loco desne?*
I'm crazy, aren't I?

DOCTOR: *Eei, te vagy a Klon ga arimasu.*
Nope, you're a clone.

YOU: *Der Klon desyo?!*
A clone?!

DOCTOR: *Si.*
Yes.

YOU: *Der Klon ga ja'nai, demo ano hito wa der Klon desyo!*
I'm not a clone, but that guy is!

INSULTS

As a rough-and-tumble, tough-as-nails detective in the Advanced Technological Dystopia, you're going to need to be able to spit out virulent language with impeccable timing in the perpetrator's native tongue. This will indicate that you know exactly what is going on and are not to be trifled with.

Cityspeak incorporates all the really good insults and curse words of all the languages—a sort of multicultural vulgarity stew. Feel free to add your own!

Zakkenayo!   (Japanese) Sort of like "Fuck off!" in English.

Tu madre!   (Spanish) "Your mother!"

Shisse!   (German) "Shit!" Good for saying to yourself when you screw something up.

Mes couilles sur ton nez, ça te fait des jolies lunettes?   (French) "Do my testicles on your nose make pretty glasses for you?"

Bukkoroshite yaru!   (Japanese) Literally, "I am going to hit you until you die."

the hacker

"If I wanted your help,
I would have pressed F1."

—EVILZUG

DISCLAIMER: For the record, I am not a hacker. I do not want
to be a hacker, and I don't care if you're a hacker. Go sneer about
it on Slashdot.

The hacker character ranges from mental kung-fu giant to intro-
verted self-absorbed weirdo. The actual business of "hacking"
basically consists of typing and looking annoyed. A hacker can be anyone, male or female. Even little girls (like Ed from *Cowboy Bebop*) can
be formidable hackers. They run the gamut from hopelessly geeky
(Max Cohen) to stylish and sexy (Neo). Whatever route you plan to
take, here are some tips for achieving hackerdom.

characteristics
of a hacker

Junk Food: Whatever you do, don't eat healthy. Proper hackers will spend at least 30 percent of their time with orange Cheetos fingers. Jolt cola shall be thy water. When not consuming pure unadulterated trash, you must eat Asian food. Chinese, Japanese, Thai . . . whatever. If Asian food is not available, you may eat pizza or Mexican.

Respect Information: This is your domain. What the information *actually is* does not matter; it's the MacGuffin. The point is, you either want it, you have it, and/or you have to keep it from getting out. Information is currency; there is no more point to hard cash. If a computer thinks you're rich, you're rich. If it thinks you're Jimmy Hoffa, you're dead. Everything is perception and perspective.

Omniscience: You are all-knowing. You and your computer can search through terabytes upon terabytes of information and instantly pluck out whatever you need. Is there a helicopter sitting there? Download. Lost in the sewers of Calcutta? Download.

The Cult of the Small Metallic Object: At any time and for any reason, you can do magic shit with a paper clip. Is there a train about to hit you? Bust out the paper clip and short the switch. Need to make a phone call? Beer top should do nicely.

Antisocial Skills: Spending time with your computer and not with other people takes a toll. In social situations involving members of the opposite sex you can be a bit awkward or naive. You should be silent and cool to cover up your lack of social graces. Or lack of acting talent. Not mentioning any names.

The Handle: Your identity must remain a secret—just like a superhero. In cyberspace you will be known only by your handle. You must choose this wisely. It should be intimidating but not over-the-top or heavy-handed. LordDeathCypher is a bit much— especially if your balls haven't dropped. You can even be ironic and go with something like CleverNickname.[40] You should also not use names that have been used already or do confusing variations on another person's handle. Be your own hacker. Don't do anything cute. If your friend Chip's handle is PitViper, don't be CobraCommander. And no numbers in the handle. Have some self-respect.

Hubris of the Hacker: You are the master ninja of the metaverse. There is nothing that you cannot accomplish by assembling a team of other info-ninjas. You have real ultimate power. Nothing can stop you!

Oh, Wait: You have a problem. The plan isn't working. Something has gone wrong. The mission is in jeopardy. . . . Oh, no, wait. You hacked right through it . . . because you are a ninja. Phew. Good thing you are such a good hacker.

---

[40] Wil Wheaton has already beaten you to this one. Burn.

how l337 are you?

That baby was:

> a) cute
> b) annoying
> c) pwn3d

Score: What kind of noob takes a quiz to test his 1337ness? stfu.

how to dress

If you plan on leaving the house, you're going to have to make yourself presentable. There are a lot of options available for a hip hacker such as yourself. Here are a few necessary objects:

- **Cool Jacket:** I personally prefer the motorcycle-racing-jacket look, but you can go for the leather trench if you don't mind the risk of looking too Goth. If you need to hide a shotgun, this might be a good option. But for sheer coolness go motorcycle jacket.

- **Weapon:** Samurai sword is the best choice, especially for females.

- **Jacks:** In case you want to plug your PS9 into your head or open doors like R2-D2.

- **Kneepads for No Reason:** Seriously, I dunno. Everyone else is doing it.

- **Really Big Shoes:**
  This will help you with . . . looking futuristic. And maybe you can hide your smack in there.

- **Old-School Round Goggles:** In case you get computer juice in your eyes.

- **Interesting Hair:**
  Blue, green, spiky, Mohawk, wires and tubes, whatever. . . .

- **Belt to Hang Things From:** Try to keep the Batman factor to a minimum here. You don't need, like, six things hanging from your belt. One is okay. One plus a gun.

i, replicant

> "Is this testing whether I'm a Replicant
> or a lesbian, Mr. Deckard?"
>
> —RACHAEL, *BLADE RUNNER*

A replicant is an artificial person. Replicants aren't born, they're grown by the Tyrell Corporation. They were never children, and they don't have parents. They have fake belly buttons. Think about it.

how to tell if you are a replicant

Replicants are sometimes given memory implants in order to trick them into doing whatever they were created to do. You may be a replicant and not even know it!

- Go look at yourself in the mirror. Do your irises glow like a cat's?

- Do you have a lot of really old pictures in your apartment? A few . . . too many?

- Do you own a piano? Do you remember taking lessons?

- Can you really take a punch? Replicants are tougher than normal people. Do you keep going even if someone breaks your fingers? Can you lose a few teeth and still drink whiskey?

- Is there a strangely dressed man who works for the police department following you around? Does he know what you dream about?

Since replicants—particularly the Nexus 6 variety—tend to occasionally wig out and kill a lot of people, they've been banished to the mining colonies and are not allowed to set foot on Earth under penalty of death. The only accurate way to tell for sure if you are a replicant is to take the Voight-Kampff Test. The problem with taking this test is that if you fail, they shoot you. This is sort of not cool.

what is the voight-kampff test?

The Voight-Kampff (V-K) Test is like a really accurate, very complex lie detector test. Replicants are programmed to exhibit emotional responses but do not have fully developed emotions of their own. Therefore, they do not react the same way as humans do to questions designed to provoke an emotional response. For example, if you ask a human to tell you the good things he remembers about his mother, he will probably tell you some cute stories about his childhood, whereas a replicant might shoot you in the face. Chances are you'll notice the difference right away.

According to Deckard, it usually takes about thirty to forty questions to determine whether or not the subject is a replicant, providing the replicant doesn't kill you before the end of the test. The V-K machine measures iris contractions and analyzes chemicals being released from the body. Smoking does not affect the test. The actual content of the answers is evaluated by the person who is administering the test. The administrator looks for indications that the subject is not as mature and/or knowledgeable as they should be based on their appearance—not knowing what a tortoise is and so on. Reaction time is a factor.

If you are a replicant with memory implants, the variation between your responses and those of a real human will be less dramatic. This is because the V-K questions are designed to provoke an empathetic response. Not unlike a child who is just learning about the world, a newborn replicant that has simply been programmed to smile will not have time to develop such an advanced emotion as empathy. But you with your implanted life experience will have much more realistic reactions. You may even experience authentic emotions.

Emotions are considered dangerous for replicants. They are designed with a four-year life span to prevent them from developing their own organic emotional responses. It is not known whether or not this fail-safe is programmed into replicants that have memory implants.

TIP: It seems worthwhile to note that Deckard (who may or may not be a replicant, depending on whom you talk to) had an apparent lack of empathy. His job involved mercilessly "retiring" replicants, and he was particularly unsympathetic to Rachael at first. If you have a similar disposition, it might be a good idea to test yourself with a V-K machine.

clones

Clones are similar to replicants in that they are both artificially grown humanoids, but there is a difference. A clone is not genetically superior to its parent organism. It is simply a copy. Cloning as we know it today is just asexual reproduction. The clone is technically just the identical twin of the original organism. What becomes messy is when there can be a copy made of a full-grown adult, memories and all.

HOW TO TELL IF YOU'VE BEEN CLONED

- Is there a strange person who looks just like you in your house?

- Is your wife/husband/partner really confused? Do they ask you questions such as, "Weren't you just wearing a different outfit?" or "Again?"

- Have you recently woken up in a strange place?

- Are people trying to kill you?

If you have been cloned, you have several options:

- Make friends with your clone and work together to stop the evil people who cloned you.

- If you *are* the clone, kill the real you and assume his place.

- Share your life with the clone. Go to work every other day. Share household chores.[41]

---

[41] Unfortunately, unless the clone runs around naked, you will be doing the same amount of laundry. It's the nature of the beast. Also, you can expect the grocery bills to double.

- Each of you should date someone different and then secretly trade. Who'll know? You're identical.

TIP: Don't let your clone make a clone of him- or herself. A copy of a copy never really turns out right.

dealing with extraterrestrials

Police: "Sir, are you classified as human?"
Korben Dallas: "Negative. I am a meat Popsicle."
—*The Fifth Element*

New Scientist magazine reported in August 2004 that scientists are estimating that contact with some sort of alien civilization will be made within the next twenty years. This may or may not be good news, because there appear to be only two kinds of aliens in the universe: (1) aliens that want to kill us, and (2) aliens that want to patronize us.

That's about it. You have your occasional sarcastic or silly alien (e.g., Mork, Alf, Howard the Duck), but they mainly crash-land or get sent here in exile.

So what will we do when aliens arrive?

The first thing that you should do is attempt to determine which variety of alien you're dealing with.

For the most part, any alien race that contacts the government first is bad news. Nice aliens always seem to land someplace where they can be discovered by a kid or a widow or something. That way it's more dramatic when they're misunderstood by some evil government men with guns and helicopters and whatnot.

TIP: Whatever reaction the military and/or government has to the alien, do the opposite. If they want to capture and dissect it, help it escape. If they invite it to dinner or tell you that it has amazing potential for humanity (read: kick-ass bioweapons), you should probably kill it immediately.

recognizing a killer alien

Killer aliens come in several varieties:

- Stealth aliens (body snatchers, puppet masters)

- Insectile psycho killers

- Military invaders

- Mysterious substances that turn out to be aliens

Unless you're dealing with a stealth killer, it should be fairly obvious which variety you are dealing with.

STEALTH ALIENS: These aliens are sneaky. Maybe they are shape-shifters like in *The Thing,* or maybe they like to burrow inside your head and hang out in there. There are body snatchers that make copies of you and take your place in society, and there are also gross green killer aliens that have really realistic costumes and pretend to be friendly. Stealth aliens may even have already conquered Earth and are using the media to keep us down.[42] You never know.

> **TIP:** If your friend (who looks a lot like a professional wrestler) wants you to try on some ugly-ass '80s sunglasses because they'll allow you to see that aliens have conquered the planet, just do it. Don't make him kick your ass for, like, seven minutes first. "Why, you dirty motherfucker!"

[42] Obey. Buy this book. It makes a great gift. Send cash.

INSECTILE PSYCHO KILLERS: This is the sort of alien that scares me the most. You can't talk to them; you can't reason with them; and unless you blow them out of the air lock or shoot one in the brain, you can never really be sure they're dead. Also, face huggers are fucking scary.

There's no really effective way to deal with an outbreak of this kind of alien, but here are some tips on staying alive long enough to escape:

1. Find out who the company has sent to sabotage the mission. Keep in mind that it may be a hobbit or the guy from *Mad About You.*

2. Don't go investigating stuff by yourself.

3. Pack flamethrowers, motion detectors, and grenades. Bring a lot of people. If you're the last adult to survive, you'll make it.

4. Save the cat. Aliens apparently don't eat cats. Maybe they're terrified of cats.

5. Never whine. Aliens kill people who whine.

6. Don't forget to look above and below you. Try to do this *before* you find a bunch of alien slime. Whatever you do, don't stick your hand in it then slowly look up.

7. Mind the acidy blood.

8. Don't sleep.

MILITARY INVADERS: This type of alien attacks the planet for its resources. Maybe they've exhausted their planet in the same way that we're exhausting ours. This is probably the sort of alien that we would be if we found an idyllic planet full of good topsoil and clean air.[43]

Can you blame them?

(For tips on thwarting an alien invasion, see the chapter "How to Stop an Alien Invasion" in Part IV.)

MYSTERIOUS SUBSTANCES THAT TURN OUT TO BE ALIENS: Here's the deal: If there is a substance that consumes everything in its path, get out of its path. And if teenagers come up to you and tell you about it, believe them. Teenagers are sort of weird, but they're not totally nuts.

The other variety of alien that you are likely to encounter (when we make contact) sometime within the next two decades is the . . .

patronizing alien

Now, I'm sure you've seen movies that feature the patronizing alien, and maybe you didn't feel very patronized. That's only because they're really good at it. Here are some categories of patronizing aliens:

- **The Ambassador:** Sent to Earth to make contact with our species.

- **The Accidental Tourist:** Whoops, got left behind!

- **The Interstellar Rotary Club:** Nifty, I've always wanted to see another planet.

---

[43] Mars may just need women. Jury is still out.

THE AMBASSADOR: The ambassador alien is usually very curious about humanity. It will probably appear to be less than intelligent—but don't let that fool you. It realizes that we are the primitive species (what with our bellicose nature and all), and sooner or later, it's going to let you know.

If you are unlucky enough to pick up one of these aliens, the best advice I can give you is not to get too emotionally attached to it. Either the government is going to kill it and dissect it or it's going to knock you up and go back to its own planet. Either way, sucks for you.

> **WARNING:** The ambassador alien might be a supreme being who has been sent down to give us a message.[44] If the message is something positive—like end all war or you will be destroyed—listen to the guy. If the message is that your date will be ten minutes late in meeting you at the museum, he's not an alien after all. He is your butler and you are a fucking nut.

THE ACCIDENTAL TOURIST: Maybe this alien was part of an anthropology exhibition. It was out there collecting samples of something or other, and the flying saucer left. Whoops. This type of alien will probably play dumb and then try to contact its buddies on the sly. It might have some sort of time limit for how long it can stay on Earth and remain healthy. If McDonald's or Coca-Cola has a significant financial interest in your new pet alien, you may want to try giving it a Coke. You never know. Coke might just be *magic*.[45]

---

[44] Beware the Jesus allegory, for it is so played.
[45] Where's my check?

THE INTERSTELLAR ROTARY CLUB: These aliens are always picking people up and dropping them off. I say, go with them. Why not? They don't want to eat your brains or enslave you, they just want to put you in a zoo or form a committee and ask you stupid questions. Admit it: That would make you feel sort of important. Or maybe they feel it's time to share their infinite knowledge with us lowly apes. Either way, it works out for you.

Another variation is the alien that tries to pick you up in a pub, then turns out to be a rather impressive political figure. You should definitely go. Bring your pet mice.

Sometimes making contact with the aliens can prove to be difficult. The infinitely wise can't just land on the White House lawn and pop the hatch. They like to buzz your house and make your vacuum cleaner go by itself. Try tapping out a few notes on the synth and see if anything happens.

robots

O ne of the most interesting aspects of robot/human interaction is the so-called uncanny valley, a term coined by the Japanese roboticist Masahiro Mori, based on his research. The *uncanny valley* refers to a phenomenon he observed when testing people's emotional reaction to robots. He found that up to a point, empathy toward the robot increased with the robot's resemblance to humans. But as the robots approached a simulacrum, the empathy experienced by the human subjects sharply dropped, turning instead to revulsion at the creepy-ass robot zombie monster. At some point we humans focus on the differences rather than the similarities. This is called the uncanny valley.

I am very, very, very freaked out by robots in the uncanny valley. Freaked. Out. I don't even like it when Haley Joel Osment acts robotic. Some examples of robots and puppets in my own personal uncanny valley are:

- Chucky (I simply will not watch Chucky movies. Will not.)

- The SimPal (*The 6th Day*)

- Howdy Doody (I don't care what you say, he's freaky.)

- Any ventriloquist doll, but especially ones that are possessed and tell you what to do

- That fucking clown from *Poltergeist*

- The creepy toys from *Toy Story*

- The nanny robot from *A.I.*

And the worst ever . . .

- The ceiling baby from *Trainspotting*. (Oh my God.)

It's my theory that the uncanny valley is responsible for our vague tendency to cast the more humanoid robots as villains. Even "good" robots that are very humanoid are not free from plotlines exposing their robot vulnerabilities, but it's hard to picture a cute little non-humanoid robot going mental.

For example:

R2-D2 is the most trustworthy robot in film history. R2 has your lightsaber, he flies your ship, he opens the door. R2 has your back. R2 is not humanoid. He doesn't even speak.

Ash (from *Alien*) is the least trustworthy robot in the history of film. Ash is gonna kill the crew.

Now, of course there are exceptions[46]—notably in the *Alien* sequels. But since you were expecting the robot to be evil, it would hardly be a good sequel if it was the same exact thing over again. Also, Bishop was arguably less realistically human than Ash because everyone knew he was a robot.

The following section contains a breakdown of different robots according to trustworthiness. As in, which robots will:

a) Not flip out and kill you with a butcher knife

b) Not "accidentally" kill or maim your family

c) Not ignore the fact that someone is killing you with a forklift[47]

What you're looking for in a robot is a useful companion that will routinely save your butt—or at least clean your house. Try to avoid anything voiced by Roddy McDowall.

totally trustworthy

R2-D2 (*Star Wars*): As mentioned above, R2 sets the standard for trustworthy robots. He's cute and he makes funny noises. Everyone loves R2.

Teddy (*A.I.*): David's Teddy is a supertoy! Personally, I love Teddy. He's another one that will save your butt. Plus, he's just so cute. There is no way Teddy is going to flip out and kill you with a machine.

---

[46] I don't care what anyone says, I don't trust that fucking robot in *Small Wonder*. She's a freak. She'll kill them all. Even the annoying girl next door.

[47] Olé!

basically good

Robot (*Lost in Space*): Robot is basically a good guy. He's sort of humanoid; he's at least got arms; and he's not short on personality. He even plays the guitar. Unfortunately, Robot can be controlled by evil Dr. Smith. To his credit, however, he is able to remain calm when being subjected to such insulting names as "Mechanized Moron," "Bubbleheaded Booby," "Demented Diode," et cetera.

Johnny 5 (*Short Circuit*): Again, not quite humanoid—pretty trustworthy. He means well, but you are never quite sure that he's not going to freak out and fry your cat with his weapons. After all, Johnny 5 was originally a military robot.

C-3PO (*Star Wars*): The most human of the robots in this section, C-3PO can honestly be called an android. And he really means well. Honest he does. But you can't trust him with anything. Seriously, would you let C-3PO babysit? No, ya wouldn't. He'd let your kid eat bleach.

bad news

Data (*Star Trek*): Trekkies, don't flip out on me. Data is the most trustworthy android out there, but . . . he's got that brother. And there was that business about the emotion chip and some unpleasantness with the Borg. Plus, you can shut him off. Sorry, but even Data is not immune. You never saw R2's evil brother show up and mess with his brain.

David (*A.I.*): Very lifelike and lovable and all, but honestly—he's totally creepy. David has severe mental problems. He's Peter Pan with a Pinocchio complex, and that's two too many fairy tales for one robot. Who would want a robot that's eternally obsessed with you? Plus, he almost drowned the annoying kid. (I can't say I blame him.)

Ash (*Alien*): Ash was so realistic, the crew didn't even know he was a robot. The only reason that they even found out he was an android was that he was the saboteur. He was programmed to let the crew die. He didn't even let it bother him. He was like, *Whatever, I'm a hobbit. Ctrl Alt Delete.*

some varieties of artificial companionship

EVIL COMPUTERS: Unsurprisingly enough, the worst of the evil untrustworthy machines are the ones that are running things. Skynet in the *Terminator* movies, for example, was really bad news all around. And HAL-9000 from *2001: A Space Odyssey* went totally bonkers and killed everyone just because it was told to lie about its mission objectives. Mother just didn't even give a crap about the *Nostromo*. Three milliseconds late on the auto-destruct? Too bad, sucker.

VERY BAD ROBOTS: Of course, some robots are meant to be bad. It's not a secret. My personal favorite evil robot is Maximilian from *The Black Hole.*

REFEREE ROBOTS: Robots make excellent umpires. They don't have any hidden biases for any team. They can be totally impartial.

Unfortunately, someone could always hack into them and give them some bias, but nobody's perfect.

The referee robot is in charge of killing anyone who gets out of line. You can't reason or argue with the robot, you just have to behave yourself.

GENERALLY USEFUL ROBOTS: Some robots are just there to be generally useful. Some examples are: Robby the Robot from *Forbidden Planet;* the aforementioned *Lost in Space* Robot; *The Black Hole's* V.I.N.Cent; C-3PO (Protocol Droid); and the NS4s. There are, of course, more specific robots that will, for example, fight a war or whatever.

WHORE-BOTS: Also known as *gynoids;* I don't think this category needs much explanation. Ask your mom.

WISECRACKING BUDDY ROBOTS: The last and most important variety of robot is the wisecracking buddy robot. Ideally, you will assemble these little guys yourself out of household objects. Or you may inherit them from the previous tenant. Wisecracking buddy robots are essential for extended spaceflight where there is little or no entertainment. Wisecracking buddy robots are very trustworthy but are prone to getting themselves into a bit of trouble. Sometimes they try things like digging holes to get back to Earth, which is not good when you're on a satellite. Also, they may have evil versions of themselves named "Timmy." Beware.

the official dystopia visitor's guide

"If you liked the book, you'll love the country."
—Israeli Tourist Bureau

N ow that you're thoroughly acquainted with the dystopia, it's time to get out of there. Here are some choice destinations to get you started.

restaurants and clubs

The White Dragon Noodle Bar (*downtown Los Angeles*) is a local favorite. Specializing in sushi and other Japanese cuisine, the White Dragon has an excellent selection of imported beer. $.

Milliways (*The End of the Universe*) serves up delicious fare in an exciting setting. The who's who of the Milky Way frequent this out-of-the-way hot spot located in a time bubble at the End of the Universe. Come for spectacular views of the explosions; stay for the food. Prices start at one penny. (Compounded interest takes care of the rest . . . ain't time travel neat?) $.

Jarre de Th (*Chiba, Night City*) has a variety of espresso drinks and a wide selection of tea in the heart of Night City. Expect to see local hustlers and artists washing down pills with double espressos on the way to the arcade. Décor is heavily mirrored and suitably lit with red neon. $.

Uncle Enzo's CosaNostra Pizza, Inc. (*nationwide*) is the best place to call for on-time pizza delivery. In fact, it's the only place to call. All pizzas delivered in thirty minutes or less. No exceptions. $$.

The Snake Pit (*Sector 4*) attracts an upper-class clientele with its nightly selection of exotic dancing and expensive drinks. Harass proprietor Taffey Lewis with a few questions about renegade replicants and receive a free drink. $$$.

Club Trash (*Detroit*) where thumping industrial sets the mood for Goth kids' night out. Popular on Devil's Night, but the owner's sort of an asshole. $$.

The Last Resort (*Venusville*) is home to a regular crowd of misfits and hooligans. Watch your wallet; pleasant company abounds but charges by the hour. Ask for Melina. $.

Blip's Arkaid (*Ottawa*) is a meeting place for young dystopic hipsters. Features coin-operated 8-bit gaming lorded over by a hilarious character actor. $.

La Fin (*Port of Marvis, Ganymede*) is a small, quiet pub with a few local regulars. The perfect setting for an awkward reunion. $.

transportation

Johnny Cab (*nationwide*) offers robot-driven taxis that service downtown and suburbs. Thanks for using Johnny Cab! $$.

Tyrell Corp. Spinner Rental (*Los Angeles*) stocks late-model, high-end spinners for all your travel needs. Spinner licenses are subject to credit check, background check, net worth assessment, and significant security deposit. Only the wealthiest need apply. $$$$$.

off-world travel

Ursa Minor Beta: Through some sort of wild coincidence, the planet Ursa Minor Beta consists almost entirely of subtropical coastline. Oddly enough, it's also perpetually Saturday afternoon just before the beach bars close. The capital, Light City, is really only called this because "swimming pools are a bit thicker on the ground there than other places." Obviously, it's a tremendously popular holiday and retirement destination. $$$.

Fhloston Paradise: A wildly popular cruise destination, the planet Fhloston has over 400 beaches. Reservations are recommended, as the floating hotels and flights to Fhloston are usually booked many months in advance. Once on board, don't forget to catch Plavalaguna at the opera hall; tuxedos provided. "Helm to 108!" $$$$.

LV-426 Adventure Safari: For the more spirited adventurer, a trip to colony LV-426 is in order. Especially recommended for single travelers with few relations. Pressure suits and hiking gear provided. Tours operated by Wayland-Yutani. $$.

Long Ago and Far Away Archeological Society: Examine some of the high-tech artifacts being discovered on planets throughout the faraway galaxies. Tours daily. Reservations recommended. $$$$.

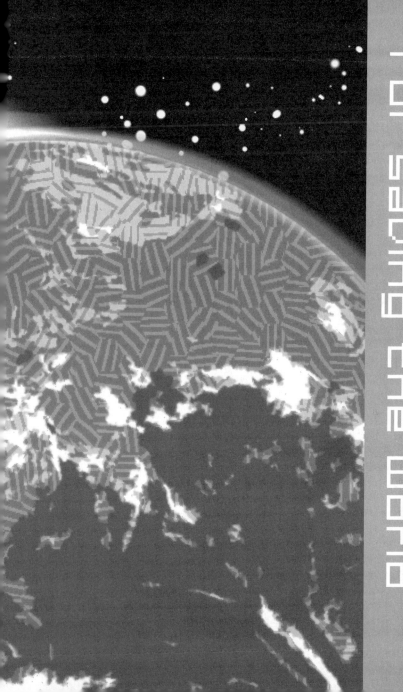

PART IV: apocalypse then: tips for saving the world

apocalypse then: tips for saving the world

> Don't Panic.
>
> —DOUGLAS ADAMS,
> *THE HITCHHIKER'S GUIDE TO THE GALAXY*

ALL THIS TALK ABOUT THE POSTAPOCALYPTIC WORLD, and we're not even there yet. So you're asking, *Isn't there anything we can do to prevent the apocalypse from happening in the first place?* Sure. You're not going to like it. Stop driving. Use public transportation. Buy a flexi-fuel car. Use biodiesel. Stop building things on farmland. Stop having so many fucking kids.

No, no, no. We meant: Isn't there anything we can do that involves rockets and guns?

Oh. Well, I'm sorry, I misunderstood. Of course there is. Part IV deals with saving the world from potentially apocalyptic disasters. Here are a few examples:

- Alien invasion

- Meteor strike

- Giant insects and other radioactive horrors

- Massive cordinated animal attack

None of these are as likely as, say, global warming, but there's no reason you shouldn't be prepared.

Good luck.

how to stop an
alien invasion

ymbolic destruction of precious landmarks. Widespread panic. Ungodly traffic. You can expect all of these and more during an alien invasion. Fortunately, all you need to repel a planetary invasion is an unlikely group of misfits thrown together by circumstance. Then you can figure out an alien race's major weakness and exploit it using whatever happens to be lying around. Groovy.

Anyone who has ever spent any amount of time playing video games can tell you one thing: Human beings, while not exceptionally powerful physically, are durable, intelligent, and versatile. Why does this matter? Well, because humans have very few major weaknesses. We're well rounded. One only has to look at the little skill bars next to the human character to see that we're average at just about everything. This means that we can adapt to take advantage of the weaknesses of others and compensate for our own with some cool technology. Crafty, aren't we? I wouldn't want to mess with us. Still, we aren't perfect.

possible human weaknesses

Too Nice: We may invite an alien race in for some good old "knowledge sharing," and while we discuss string theory, they download the go code and nuke Russia.

Too Paranoid: Shooting first may not be the best idea, but nothing surprises me about our foreign policy anymore.

Susceptible to Disease: Who knows what lethal parasites, viruses, or bacteria an alien race might have at their disposal.

Sucky Technology: Let's face it: If they can manage to get here, they're obviously more advanced than we are. We can't even get the Patriot missile to work right. Instead of attacking the mother ship, we'll probably hit a wedding.

Our Kung Fu Is Not Strong: When challenged to one-on-one combat for the fate of the human race, whom shall we send? What if Chuck Norris is busy?[48]

possible alien weaknesses

Human Diseases/Microbes: There's always a chance that once the aliens arrive, they'll all die from chicken pox without us having to lift a finger. Of course, it could go the other way around as well, and they could infect us. There's just no way to tell until they get here. Thankfully, though, we're a bunch of jerks and have a pretty hefty arsenal of genetically engineered bioweapons

[48] Fucking Chuck Norris.

with a 99.9 percent kill rate. (They are known as IDDs, or Insanely Destructive Devices.) For example, the fatality rate for a badass disease like smallpox is only 30 percent. So bring it on, alien scum.

Hack the Planet: Messing with the life-support systems of the alien invader is an excellent way to thwart an invasion. This is especially effective if they happen to be cyborgs. You could put them all to sleep or something.[49] The only concern is that actual non-Hollywood hackers don't really have computer superpowers. They're more likely to just call up Barb at the home office and pretend to be someone who has lost their password. I don't know if there has been a hacker yet who could call up the mother ship and trick them into revealing a code.

> MOTHER SHIP: Thank you for calling the Planetary Attack Hotline. This is Dweezk. How may I help you?

> HACKER: Yes, this is Captain Blarg from the 182nd Decapitation Unit. I've misplaced my log-in information.

> MOTHER SHIP: Sorry to hear that, Captain. Please enter your user name, and we'll e-mail you your password hint.

> HACKER: Yeah, 'bout that . . . you see, my computer got destroyed by one of those primitive Earthling AK-47s, so I was wondering if you could just forward that to my Hotmail account and I'll check it at the Kinkos on the way to destroy the White House.

---

[49] This apparently pisses off headquarters and they send more ships (enough for a feature-length film), so don't bank on this one unless you fancy being sexually harassed by the queen cyborg in the sequel.

MOTHER SHIP: Sure, no problem, Captain Blarg. Could you just confirm with your mother's maiden name and [*click*] . . . Captain Blarg? Are you there, sir?

Bad Music: Surprising though it may seem, this one actually has some basis in reality. For example, the navy's new ultraloud sonar may be responsible for the deaths of dozens of beached whales in Washington, Puerto Rico, and the Canary Islands.[50] Some of these whales were found hemorrhaging from the eyes and ears.

Also, the army already has a prototype sonic weapon that, when aimed directly at a person, will bring them to their knees even if they plug their ears. The weapon sends out a narrow beam of sound at up to 145 decibels—fifty times the threshold of pain. It will literally vibrate your skull. Neat! The device can use any annoying sound; one example is a baby's scream played backward.

I figure you could use this device in combination with the most overplayed song in human history—Celine Dion's "My Heart Will Go On" from the *Titanic* sound track. If that doesn't send the aliens fleeing to the silent vacuum of space, I do not know what will.

H_2O: No alien culture would be dumb enough to get in a ship and drive 100 light-years to conquer a planet that was made up mostly of a substance that is deadly poisonous to them . . . while wearing no clothes. If they were that stupid, they wouldn't have made it off their planet in the first place.

---

[50] The navy should really consider not killing all the whales with sonar, because according to *Star Trek IV*, there's going to be a violent alien probe that enjoys having really boring conversations with sea life. No comment on the odds of this actually happening.

Here are some more reasons why *Signs* is a stupid movie:

- The aliens can travel through space, but they can't break into Mel Gibson's house (or remember to bring raincoats).

- Water is "really bad" for them, and yet they appear to be just fine running through a humid, dewy cornfield in their bare asses.

- In order to remain safe, you would just need to stand in your shower—or pee on them if they grabbed you.

- Ending stolen from *The Wizard of Oz* (i.e., the Wicked Witch of the East).

- The whole "signs" thing isn't deep. It's what happens when you try real hard to be deep . . . and fail.[51]

Computer Virus: Again, this one isn't too likely. Unless Bill Gates has gotten to the aliens first, they probably have a pretty secure operating system. Besides, even if their system crashed, one would assume they had some sort of backup plan. But maybe not—what do I know? If *Independence Day* is any indication, one could steal an alien spacecraft, throw in a new seat belt, type up a computer virus on a PowerBook, and fly on up to the mother ship—where your virus will swiftly save the planet from the evil alien invaders. This, of course, means that Steve Jobs is an alien, which may explain why the Mac isn't compatible with anything here on Earth.

---

[51] I understand "what the movie is really about." It doesn't make it any less stupid. I highly suspect the theme was just there to get Mel "I Know Jesus" Gibson on board. "No, Mel, it's not a movie about aliens. It's about God and fate . . . and I'll give you twenty million dollars." "Oh, okay, where do I sign?" "Hmm. Sign . . . that's catchy."

how to save
the world

It starts with an earthquake—
birds and snakes—an aeroplane.
Lenny Bruce is not afraid.
—R.E.M., "It's the End of the World
As We Know It (And I Feel Fine)"

One could argue that there is no way to "save the planet"—that we're just doomed to destroy ourselves. The planet itself will be fine. However, eventually the sun will grow large and hot, the oceans will burn off, and ultimately, the entire planet will be consumed in fire. It's a hell of an argument, isn't it? So I guess this chapter should really be called "How to Delay the Inevitable." That's not as catchy, though.

So, anyway, maybe there's a meteor about to hit the planet, maybe Earth's orbit is about to spin out of control, maybe it's time for another ice age. Who knows? All that really matters is that you've decided to be the one to save the planet. That's great. We all admire your initiative.

Before you can begin saving the world, you need to survive the initial wave of devastation. Every potential apocalypse needs a truly righteous natural disaster to put things into perspective.

how to survive a pre-apocalyptic natural disaster

Before the actual apocalypse can occur, several incredibly devastating (but not really planet-ending) natural disasters must befall us. In order to guarantee your survival, follow these rules:

1. Try to get separated from your loving family. If you can, be sure to have just had stern words with one or more of them. This ensures that both—if not all—of you will not only survive, but be able to find each other again in the aftermath of the disaster. At that time you will have the opportunity to resolve your issues and properly appreciate each other.

2. Stay the hell away from landmarks. Here's a short list of potentially lethal landmarks to avoid: Empire State Building, Eiffel Tower, the White House, the Statue of Liberty, the Golden Gate Bridge, and Big Ben.

3. Cover yourself completely in dogs and children.

Extra Bonus Rule for Females: Be a stripper who is just trying to provide a better life for her children and who is going to school on the side. This appears to be the highest a woman can aspire to, dramatically speaking.

actually saving the damn world

The first step on the road to actually saving the world is to become a member of the elite team, handpicked by the U.S. government, that will go on a do-or-die mission to save the planet from certain destruction. We rule the world, after all—we're obviously going to be in charge of saving it. Not to mention the fact that we're probably the ones who broke it in the first place. In order to increase the probability of being chosen, you should begin modeling yourself after one of the following necessary members of any self-respecting planetary rescue squad:

> **The Scientist with the Crackpot Theory:** You're the guy who ruins Thanksgiving every year by going on and on about how we're all doomed. Little children are reminded by their parents not to mention "global warming" or "methane" once you've had something to drink. Your colleagues invite you to events only because they have to, and they roll their eyes as soon as you step away. But don't worry, it's okay. Naturally, it will turn out that you were right all along, and somber men in suits will put you on a plane. Incredibly, a guy you went to college with (who is now a general) will brief you on your top secret mission. And all this time you thought that they thought you were crazy!

> **The Asshole with an Indispensable Skill Set:** You're really, really good at something. In fact, you're just about the best there is. Except maybe there's this one thing that's been nagging at you and giving you an inferiority complex. Never mind. You're convinced that you're the best and you're just about as cocky and patronizing as humanly possible, because you know that

everyone simply *has* to put up with you. You'd never suspect that everyone secretly hates you. Don't worry about that, though; you'll be given the opportunity to redeem your horrifically one-dimensional personality by martyring yourself to save humanity. How nice.

The Reluctant Hero: You're just a regular guy, but for some reason, you have some obscure skill that makes you really important to the mission. Now, you're no hero, but you'll do what you've got to do, particularly if there's something in it for good old number one. Try not to be too reluctant or you'll end up martyring yourself along with the asshole with the indispensable skill set.

The Eccentric Foreigner: Aren't foreign people *wacky*? If you're not from the USA, you are sure to be cast as the wacky foreigner. This is because all foreign people are first of all foreign and second of all everything else. And all of them are goofy. Unless they are female, in which case foreigners all have the same sexy, no-nonsense personality. Just to recap: Male foreigner = wacky, female foreigner = sexy.[52]

The Master and the Protégé: This requires two people. The master will keep telling the protégé that he/she isn't ready and that he/she must learn control. Then the master will die, and the protégé will have to save the world. This is a good scenario for pilots or other positions that require both physical stamina and mental concentration. It will also help if you, the protégé, have recently destroyed something strategically important and fairly expensive.

[52] This leads me to wonder what the dating scene is like in other countries. Every single courtship must be like a nasty episode of *Blind Date*.

The Obligatory Hacker: For some reason, in the event of a global emergency, people who went to M.I.T. to learn how to use computers will not be able to help anyone with anything. Apparently, what the army will need is some kid who guessed the password to his school's computer system and changed his econ grade. If this is you, welcome aboard. I'm sure there will be some way to rationalize why you are even slightly useful.

Once this crack team has been assembled, you'll need a short but intense training period, and then it's off to save the world! There is no doubt going to be some kind of heartrending send-off ceremony if, indeed, it is public knowledge that you are heading off to save the planet. Once the mission is under way, there are sure to be some snags. Rest assured that whatever sort of ship or vehicle you're in will sustain as much damage as it possibly can. You'll probably need to come up with at least three totally new plans, most likely involving duct tape and the phrase "It sounds crazy, but it just might work."

> **TIP:** Build a lot of extra non-mission-critical pieces on to the vehicle that you'll be using to save the world. That way you can blow up three or four times without actually affecting the mission too much. Fuel tanks would be good. Oxygen is also not bad, because this opens up the possibility of having a dramatic "we're running out of air" sequence where one member of the team has to make it to the reserves. Locate the reserves pretty far away from the cockpit for maximum drama.

Here is some advice for making it through the mission and back home safely:

- Do not under any circumstances show a picture of your children to anyone. Do not bring along a drawing they did of you and Mommy. Above all, never tell anyone that you're "doing this for these little guys." This means certain death.

- Try not to have a long-standing conflict with anyone. If you do, circumstances will dictate that one of you must be mortally wounded—forcing both of you to use what little time you have left to resolve the issue.

- If you're one of the last three or four people left, start cracking jokes. If you're at least sort of funny and also shorter than everyone else, you're practically home free.

And finally, the single most important thing to remember when attempting to save the world: *Bring extra detonators*.

I really can't stress this enough. For every bomb that you will need, bring, like, sixty-five detonators. Stick some extra detonators in your carry-on luggage in case your checked baggage gets lost. Hide a detonator in your shoe. Put a detonator in a magnetic clip and hide it under the landing gear. Whatever it takes. Extra detonators. You heard it here first.

massive coordinated animal attack

This is the coastal town that they forgot to close down
Armageddon, come, Armageddon!
Come, Armageddon, come.

—MORRISSEY, "EVERYDAY IS LIKE SUNDAY"

veryone who has seen *The Birds* reacts the same way when they see a bunch of crows sitting on a jungle gym. Nervous. Very nervous.

But what would we actually do if the animals decided to attack? Run? Scream? Blow up a gas station?

Here are some tips for dealing with several types of massive coordinated animal attacks:

Birds: Make sure you do a good job boarding up the windows and the doors. Birds can fly quite quickly and can probably break your window if they fly into it hara-kari style. Do not venture up to the attic by yourself. Keep a few birds in a cage and watch them closely for signs. If you're really under attack, throw all your Teflon pots and pans into the oven. The vapors from burning Teflon will kill most birds.

Insects: There is not a whole lot we can do if the insects decide to rise up. Due to their small size, they can get us almost anywhere. I'd try donning a level 4 biosuit. If viruses can't get in, bugs won't be able to either, I assume. Then I'd say you're going to need about ten million gallons of Raid. Set up a Raid moat. That should hold them at least until you need to drink water or eat. Then you're in trouble.

Dogs and Cats: If our pets decide to overthrow us, we're pretty much doomed. Dogs and cats have access to the White House, and they are trusted implicitly—they're leading blind people around, for Pete's sake.

PET ATTACK COMBAT TACTICS: Immediately stock up on laser pens, flashlights, and string. Use these items as a diversion while your partner gets the vacuum cleaner. This should take care of the cats. For the remaining dogs, attempt to ask if they wanna go for a walk. In the event that they do not, find a sticklike object and throw it. When they turn their heads to watch the stick, get in the car. Remember *Cujo?* Dogs can't open car doors. No thumbs.

Badgers, Squirrels, and Raccoons: This may be the most menacing threat facing the human population today. Reports are coming in from all over the UK that the squirrels and badgers are attacking. One squirrel terrorized an entire town until someone finally shot it. In a seemingly quiet town in

England a badger knocked on one man's door in the middle of the night. When he went out to investigate, the badger leaped on him like something out of a horror movie. "My husband opened the door and the badger sat there and then, gradually, just slowly walked towards him and attacked him," the man's wife reports.[53] The badger then went on a rampage injuring five people, one of whom was walking home from a pub.

Cute animals hate us. They don't think of themselves as cute, and we're giving them low self-esteem. Plus, new data shows that every squirrel or raccoon is only one or two degrees of separation away from a highway roadkill death. That bump in the road was someone's mother, and they're reading license plates and coming for you in the night. Don't open the door.

[53] "Badger Rampage Injures Five," BBC News, May 12, 2003.

on giant insects and other mutant terrors

> "Where do I get off asking the Regular Army for help with a bunch of oversize grasshoppers?"
>
> —Colonel Sturgeon (Thomas Browne Henry),
> Beginning of the End

THEM! (1954)

Monster: Giant Radioactive Mutant Ants

Comments: This was the highest-grossing film of 1954 for Warner Bros.—which goes a long way toward explaining the radioactive trend that would follow. As far as killing the ants, the idea is to find their queen and kill her so they can't reproduce. Then, you'll have to keep them from making another queen. This is a fairly complicated task, a bit more than the Orkin Man is prepared to deal with.

GODZILLA (1956)

Monster: Godzilla

Comments: H-bomb testing awakens a huge prehistoric monster that really dislikes Japanese people. Eventually, Godzilla would "turn good" and start protecting the people of Japan from various monsters (all I see is sweaty Japanese men in rubber suits). Some examples:

> **Megalon (1973):** A huge bug thing with the top of the Chrysler Building for arms is awoken from the depths of Seatopia (a land under the sea where the population is trapped in some kind of perpetually somber variety show) by some undersea residents who are pissed off about nuclear testing.

> **Mechagodzilla (1974):** Alien Godzilla imposter is sent down to Earth to kick some ass. (Godzilla has definitely entered a baroque period, don't you think?)

THE AMAZING COLOSSAL MAN (1957)

Monster: Huge Oversized Mutant Man

Comments: A test pilot is exposed to—you guessed it—radiation and begins to grow. Eventually, he gets a little funny in the head, grabs his girlfriend, and goes to hang out at the Hoover Dam for the movie's climax. Yep. He's huge, but since he's just a big old radioactive human, you can shoot him with a big old depleted uranium bullet. Problem solved.

BEGINNING OF THE END (1957)

Monster: Giant Mutant Grasshoppers[54]

Comments: This film has Peter Graves in it, which is cool, and takes place in Chicago, which is hilarious. The idea is that agricultural experiments have resulted in huge locusts that eat everything in their path, and (sure enough) Chicago and its many landmark buildings happen to be right in the way. For some reason—not explained in the film—the giant grasshoppers choose to attack giant postcards of Chicago and leave the real city alone. Not sure what this means.

[54] Insects cannot grow up to 1,000 times their size or they would be 1,000 times their weight and therefore collapse. So you can cancel that order for 6,000 cans of Raid.

TEENAGERS FROM OUTER SPACE (1959)

Monster: Giant Alien Lobster

Comments: Here's where it starts to get not just stupid, but *awe-inspiringly* stupid. Alien teenagers want to use Earth as a breeding ground for these huge lobsters they call "Gargons" (presumably, someone has been flipping through Edith Hamilton's *Mythology*). Some stuff happens on the screen for about ninety minutes, and then the plan is foiled. My thoughts on defeating the giant lobster: Giant lobster pot, giant butter, giant lemon.

THE GIANT GILA MONSTER (1959)

Monster: Giant Gila Monster

Comments: "Leg up!"[55] No, but seriously, folks—this movie is special because it contains a huge mutant freak monster that gets blown up real good by a teenager in a hot rod. No mad scientists, no aliens, no nuclear war on the dance floor—just plain old rock and roll. Golly!

THE KILLER SHREWS (1959)

Monster: Big (Killer) Shrews[56]

Comments: Aside from not knowing what a shrew actually is, this sounds terrifying. Maybe it's the "Killer" part of the title, I'm not sure. While watching the movie, I learned that a shrew is a collie wearing a rubber mask. I am no longer terrified.

---

[55] Keep circulating the tapes.

[56] I thought maybe this had something to do with Shakespeare. Revenge for *Kiss Me Kate* or something. Maybe Kate gets a posse of shrews, and they waste John Wayne's ass. Apparently not. Huge letdown for me.

NIGHT OF THE LEPUS (1972)

Monster: Huge killer mutant bunny rabbits (I swear to God)

Comments: What can you say about this film? Yes, the filmmakers were serious. It even has Janet Leigh and DeForest (Bones from *Star Trek*) Kelley. It isn't available on video, but you can see a clip of it playing at the oracle's house in *The Matrix* (see "How to Recognize a Dream World" in Part I). I don't know what kind of drugs these people were on when they decided to make this movie, but I really want some. I mean, can you imagine the production meetings? I guess it was based on a book, which means someone actually took the time to write a book about huge killer mutant bunny rabbits—a serious book, with a "moral" about pest control and animal testing. Then some other people thought it would make a good movie. Then they found someone to pay for it, direct it, write it . . . it's jaw-dropping, really. Just picture a production assistant smearing fake blood on a rabbit's mouth. Rabbits are herbivores. Rabbits are not—oh God, I can't even handle it. Worst movie . . . ever.[57]

---

[57] Or not. I don't want to debate this. Don't send letters. Some movies suck so powerfully that the sucking reaches infinity and therefore can no longer be ranked. It's the event horizon of the black hole of suck; certain movies pass it, and then no one can say for certain what happens next.

epilogue:
mr. apocalypse

"If I was the last man on Earth and you was the
last woman, I would go to bed with a bush."
—ARCHIE BUNKER (CARROLL O'CONNER), *ALL IN THE FAMILY*

What if you really were the last man on Earth? What if you were the last woman? Who from our dreary pop culture would be the best choice for a postapocalyptic companion? Feeling like a great investigative journalist, I asked some people this very question. Here is a sampling of their answers:

IF CIVILIZATION FALLS TOMORROW, WHO WOULD YOU CHOOSE TO SPEND THE APOCALYPSE WITH?

- "Angelina Jolie. Easy. Next Question." Pete, age 35

- "Your mom. No, Leeloo from *The Fifth Element*." Tom, age 25

- "Clint Eastwood. I feel safe with Clint Eastwood." Brooke, age 25

- "Johnny Depp. No. Wait. Andrew Dan-Jumbo from *While You Were Out*. He's so beautiful. And handy." Tracy, age 23

- "Eddie Izzard. He's a transvestite d'action." Caitlin, age 19

- "Well, if I can't have Mystique from *X-Men*, then someone with multiple personality disorder, so you'd never know who you'd be talking to next. You know. Sybil." Mike, age 35

- "Superman. Wait. No. Super*girl*. Better." Godfrey, age 7

The Jolie Factor: Hands down, the most popular response was Angelina Jolie. Practically every other answer was Angelina Jolie. They didn't even need to think about it. This leads me to believe that she is an alien and that she's amassing an army of dim-witted men. Expect her to take over the planet at any time.

THE TOP FIVE BEST MEN TO SPEND THE APOCALYPSE WITH

1. Korben Dallas (Bruce Willis) from *The Fifth Element*—Three words: orange tank top.

2. Mad Max (Mel Gibson)—He's moody and sort of annoying but very resilient.

3. Indiana Jones (Harrison Ford)—You may ask, *Why not Han Solo?* Easy. No Ph.D.

4. Bill Murray—Bill Murray is so hilarious. So freaking hilarious.

5. Bobby Flay—Because I bet he could make rat taste not like rat. Think about it.

**SPECIAL HAPPY LUCKY BONUS: NUMBER ONE PERSON
TO WITNESS THE APOCALYPSE WITH**

George Carlin—Because he'd be so fucking joyous about the whole thing.

TOP FIVE WORST MEN TO SPEND THE APOCALYPSE WITH

1. David Brent from *The Office*

2. Louie De Palma from *Taxi* (Louie actually built a survival bunker in an episdode of *Taxi,* so you know there's a chance . . .)

3. Private Hudson

4. James Lipton

5. Woody Allen (not that I don't love Woody Allen, but I think you understand my thinking here)

other bests and worsts

Best Song for an End-of-the-World Montage: "We'll Meet Again," Vera Lynn

Best Song That Is Actually About the Apocalypse: "It's the End of the World As We Know It (And I Feel Fine)," R.E.M.

Best Song to Play If You'd Like to Confuse a Hovering Alien: "Come Together," The Beatles

Best Robot to Spend the Apocalypse With: Teddy from *A.I.*

Best Ambassador to Send to the Alien Craft: Conan O'Brien

Worst Ambassador to Send to the Alien Craft: Rush Limbaugh

Most Hilarious Ambassador to Send to the Alien Craft: Boy George

Best Sports Commentator for the Thunderdome: Bob Costas

Best Humans to Explain the Human Reproductive System to the Aliens: Trey Parker and Matt Stone

Worst Human to Explain the Human Reproductive System to the Aliens: Michael Jackson

News Anchor Who Will Last the Longest Without Stopping to Pee During Continuous Coverage of the Apocalypse: Peter Jennings, ABC

Best Human to Announce That the Aliens Have Arrived: Steven Wright

Worst Human to Announce That the Aliens Have Arrived: Anne Heche

And finally . . .

Best Human to Overthrow the Planet and Become Our Omnipotent Overlord for All Eternity: Al Franken (why not?)

about the experts

Thomas Mannino (a.k.a. "Evilzug"): Mr. Mannino graduated in 2002 from Emerson College in Boston. He is currently employed as a Flash game programmer, is the Webmaster of several Web sites, and is the co-host and co-founder of EndGameRadio, the Internet's best all-gaming-culture radio network. You can find Tom at: www.evilzug.com, www.tommannino.com, or www.endgameradio.com. Tom would like to inform you that you are in no danger of contracting SARS. He is the master of the Internet.

Michael Chen (a.k.a. "Smart Neighbor"): Originally from Boston, Mr. Chen blatantly wears a Red Sox hat while living next door to me in the Wrigleyville neighborhood of Chicago. He currently attends Northwestern University, where he is a Ph.D. student in the pharmacology and toxicology curriculum of the Integrated Graduate Program in Life Sciences. Mike studied biology and biotechnology at Worcester Polytechnic Institute (B.S., '99) and then conducted research on the modeling of thrombosis using synthetic blood vessels in the laboratory of William Abbott at Harvard Medical School. His thesis research involves developing a mouse model of neurogenic cystitis for characterizing interactions between mast cells and bladder cells during the inflammatory response.

Daniel Swibel (a.k.a. "Postapocalyptic Rebel"): Mr. Swibel graduated in 2002 from the Theatre School of DePaul University. An award-winning filmmaker and playwright, he made his first feature while still in high school. Set in a postapocalyptic world of his own creation, *Darquetime* is the stuff of legend. Danny offers his ten-plus years of postapocalyptic costuming expertise and invaluable insight into the *Planet of the Apes* series.

Edgar Marco (a.k.a. "Captain Information"): Edgar Marco, aside from being my father, has been an electrician with Union Local 701 for over thirty-five years. Mr. Marco (as we call him) has installed many of the generators that the Chicagoland area will be using once the apocalypse is truly nigh. He is also invaluable for his knowledge of the carburetor, an archaic car part most people my age have never even seen.

acknowledgments

I understand now why books have all these acknowledgments. Book writing causes you to be insufferably selfish, egomaniacal, and annoying. I now have no friends.

Thankfully, I have this section with which to get them back.

Thanks to Mom and Dad for making me food during writing benders at their house and otherwise just being wonderfully supportive. Thank you to Caitlin, my little sister, for putting up with me and my cups-in-the-living-room problem. Thanks to Gizmo the cat for sitting on all available paper. Thanks: Michael Chen, Tom Mannino, Daniel Swibel, Brian Urban, everyone at EndGame Radio, Deuce of Clubs, and Wagner, and to the vitaminwater girls: Mari Camplin, Brooke Sylvester, and Tracy Tran.

Special thanks to Mike Staley for allowing me access to his movie collection. I'd like to take this opportunity to let the world know that Mike is currently all out of bubble gum.

I love New York:

Thank you, Adam Chromy, wonder agent, for your invaluable advice and for helping me with absolutely everything I needed. You are a rock star.

Thank you, Beth Bracken, Best Friends Forever. I do not know what I expected from an editor, but it certainly wasn't a buddy. You are the best.

Thanks to Dominic Bugatto, Sammy Yuen Jr., Joel Avirom, and Jason Snyder.

Thanks to Tricia Boczkowski, Lauren Forte, Jen Bergstrom, and everyone else at Simon Spotlight Entertainment. Your hospitality and general awesomeness are very much appreciated.

about the author

Meghann Marco grew up outside of Chicago, in a loving family environment relatively free from dysfunction. Were it not for hearing the words *penis breath* in the movie *E.T.*, she would have probably turned out all right.

"I thank God daily that future generations will be spared the gratuitous physical violence of Han Solo shooting first," the traumatized author says.

Meghann invites fans to stay tuned for *Field Guide to the Apocalypse: Special Edition*, in which the word *fuck* will be replaced with little pictures of walkie-talkies.

This is her first book.

www.meghannmarco.com or www.apocalypsefieldguide.com.